AN ILLUSTRATED HISTORY
OF THE
CHINESE IN AMERICA

AN ILLUSTRATED HISTORY
OF THE
CHINESE IN AMERICA

RUTHANNE LUM MCCUNN

DESIGN ENTERPRISES OF SAN FRANCISCO

for two very special people
my mother & my husband

Library of Congress Catalog Card Number: 79-50114

International Standard Book Number
Hardback: 0-932538-01-0
Paperback: 0-932538-02-9

Printed in U.S.A.

Front Cover: Three Chinese men in Silver City, Idaho.

Back Cover: A Chinese family in San Francisco in the late 1800's.

DESIGN ENTERPRISES OF SAN FRANCISCO
P.O. Box 27677
San Francisco, California, 94127

Acknowledgments

This book has gone through many phases. During each phase, I have been fortunate in receiving help from both friends and strangers who have been generous with their time and talents.

The initial idea for writing the history of the Chinese in America for young people was prompted by Antoinette Metcalf.

I was encouraged to continue probing for information by my students' perceptive, relentless questions and their eagerness to read everything I wrote for them.

During the initial drafts of the book, I received important, insightful criticism from Dic Fritz, Robin Grossman, Hoi Lee, Gale Ow, and Ellen Yeung.

The completed manuscript was carefully checked for accuracy by H. Mark Lai, historian. I am deeply indebted to him for sharing his knowledge and giving so much of his valuable time to a stranger.

I am also grateful for the careful proofreading of the manuscript by Lynda Preston and Stan Sargent.

Many people provided me with invaluable help in searching out the appropriate photographs in this book. These people include: the librarians at Bancroft Library; Gordon Lew, editor, East West Journal; Laverne Dicker, photo archivist, the California Historical Society; Puanani Kini and Irma Tam Soong at the Hawaii Chinese History Center; Agnes C. Conrad, State Archivist, State of Hawaii; Jim Davis, photo archivist, Idaho State Historical Society; Mrs. Perham, owner, New Almaden Museum; Ben Hazard and Dorothy Delahusay at the Oakland Museum; Cathy Flynn and Mark Sexton at the Peabody Museum; Gladys Hansen, San Francisco City Archivist, San Francisco Public Library; Peter Louis at the United Front Press; Phil Choy, Sister M. Alfreda Elsensohn, Ed Gray, Ed Sue, Alex Ross, Robin Grossman, and John Roussel.

Finally, but most especially, I wish to thank my husband. Without his considerable talents and hours of labor, this book would not exist.

Contents

Preface

America is a nation of immigrants. Even the first people, the Native Americans, are believed to have migrated from another continent, Asia. The history of America is therefore a history of the different ethnic groups - where they came from and why; their contributions, hardships and achievements; their assimilation as well as their preservation of what is unique to their cultural group; and their lives today.

Though the history of America is incomplete unless it includes all its ethnic groups, the history of the Chinese in America has remained largely an untold story. Perhaps this oversight is due to the fact that Chinese-Americans still number less than a million in a nation of 220 million. Nevertheless, their influence and contributions over the last 130 years have had a profound effect on the course of American history.

It is therefore my privilege and pleasure to share the lives of these hardy American pioneers with you. May you be as enriched from the reading of this history of our Chinese forbears as I have been from the research and writing of it.

Ruthanne Lum McCunn
San Francisco, Calif.

First Asian Americans

The Asian and American continents are on opposite sides of the world. They are separated by the Pacific Ocean but many thousands of years ago, they were joined together by a narrow strip of land near the North Pole. This bridge between the continents was called the Bering Straits.

Historians believe that people from Asia walked across this strip of land. They settled in different parts of the two American continents and became the first Asian Americans. People had not learned to record history when this migration took place but there are many signs to show that it really happened.

1.1 Asians walked across the Bering Straits.

One clue may be found in the early art of Peru in South America. Some of the ancient paintings have drawings of a tiger that only lives on the Asian continent.

Another piece of evidence is that both the early Chinese and the early Indians of Mexico believed jade to be magic. They carved the stone in much the same way and used it as offerings to their gods.

They also had the same unusual burial ceremony for their nobles and the rich. They painted a piece of jade red. Then they placed the painted stone in the dead person's mouth before burial.

Archaeologists have also found very old Chinese objects in Victoria, British Columbia. These objects prove that Chinese either visited or lived in Canada centuries ago.

The first written proof of Chinese in America can be found in the Great Chinese Encyclopedia. The historian Ma Tuan-Lin wrote that a Buddhist priest named Hui Shen arrived in British Columbia, Canada in 458 A.D. He then traveled down the coast until he reached Mexico.

There are Spanish records that show Chinese worked as ship builders in Lower California between 1571 and 1746.

In 1769, when the Spanish explorer Portola camped in Elysian Park, south of the Los Angeles river, he found a village called Yangna, which is a Chinese name. The business in that village was the boiling of herbs for the healing of the sick. It is believed that Chinese from Mexico came north and founded the village.

The first dated records in the United States show the arrival of Chinese in 1785. At that time, three Chinese seamen were left stranded in Baltimore, Maryland when their captain decided to stay and marry a local woman.

From then on, American records show that Chinese continued coming to the United States each year as merchants, servants and students. However, they did not start to come in great numbers until after gold was discovered in California in 1848.

The Chinese who came to the "Golden Mountains" (as they called California) soon discovered that making a fortune was not as easy as they had hoped. They had to endure many hardships. Despite these hardships, they continued to come.

In order to understand why the Chinese came to America, it is necessary to see what kinds of lives they were leaving behind in China.

Foreigners in China

China had a highly developed civilization as early as the ancient Greeks and Romans. It had a very structured society headed by an Emperor who was like a King. Under the Emperor were aristocrats and magistrates who governed the country. Most of the people, however, were peasants who had to work very hard just to survive.

China believed itself to be self-sufficient. It grew or made almost everything the people needed including many luxurious products.

Occasional travelers and merchants from Europe visited China before the 1500's. They took Chinese products back home with them. When the European people saw the beautiful silks, porcelains and lacquerware and tasted the delicious teas, they wanted more.

The European merchants wanted to satisfy their customers. The Chinese merchants were anxious to trade too, but during the fifteenth and sixteenth centuries the Chinese government would not allow the European ships to dock in China. The government was afraid of foreign influence. It didn't want to risk change.

In order to trade with the Europeans, some Chinese merchants filled their boats (called junks) with merchandise and sailed to the Philippine Islands to trade with the Spanish who sailed there from Mexico.

Finally, in 1757, the Chinese government agreed to open one port to the foreigners for trade, the port of Kwangchow (Canton). However, the government forced very high taxes and strict rules on the European traders.

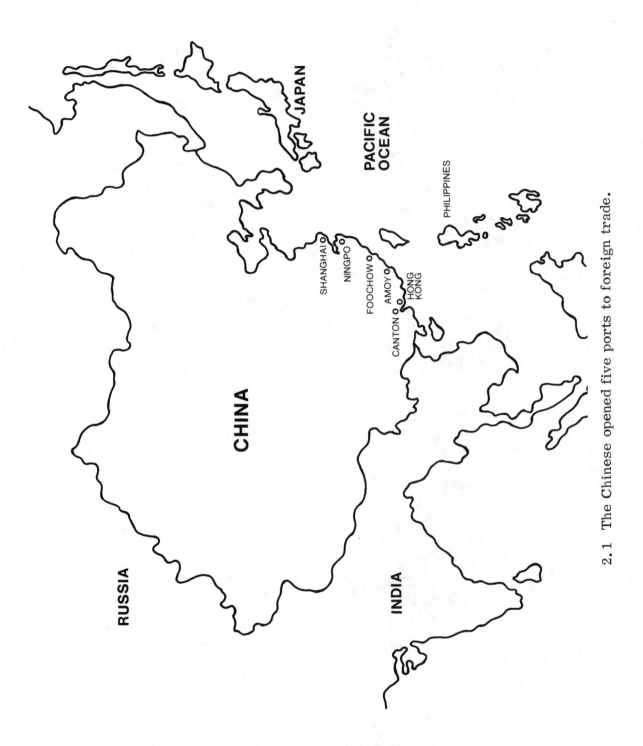

2.1 The Chinese opened five ports to foreign trade.

2.2 The European factories in Canton.

The foreign merchants had to trade through large Chinese companies called Hongs. While the ships could dock in the port, the merchants were not allowed into the walled city of Kwangchow; and they were not allowed to gather in groups of more than ten.

The biggest problem for the merchants was that the Chinese people were not interested in most of the products from Europe and America. It wasn't good business for the foreign merchants to buy from the Chinese without selling them something in return. They kept wondering what they could bring to China to sell.

Finally, the Portuguese found something new to try. They brought in opium, a powerful drug made from poppies. When opium is smoked, it makes the person dream that everything is happy and wonderful. Life for many of the Chinese people was often unbearably hard. Opium made them forget their troubles. It therefore became more and more popular.

The opium trade grew. All the other Western countries, especially Britain, started bringing opium to China.

The Chinese government did not like the opium trade. Too much opium made the users so sick and weak that they were unable to work or do anything except take more of the drug. Also, the Chinese merchants paid for the opium with silver. There was too much silver leaving the country.

The Chinese government passed a law in 1796 to stop the sale of opium. The law was not very effective because corrupt Chinese officials and Chinese smugglers helped the European merchants smuggle opium into China. The opium problem became worse.

Alarmed, the Chinese government passed a law in 1838 that made the growing, selling or smoking of opium punishable by death. Chinese government ships started seizing and destroying all opium shipments to China. In fact, there is still a place in Kwangchow, preserved as a national monument because Commissioner Lui burned tens of thousands of pounds of seized opium there.

The British grew opium in India, a part of the British Empire, so they became the chief opium traders. They needed the Chinese market to sell to. The British merchants had already been impatient with the trade restrictions for years. Now they were furious at their loss of cargoes and profits.

Finally, the bad feelings between China and Britain burst out in a sea battle off the coast of Kwangtung Province, near Kwangchow, in 1839. This was the beginning of the Opium War.

China was no longer the strong, self-sufficient country that it had been when the Europeans had first arrived. It had not kept up with modern technological advances. Worse, its once powerful government had become corrupt and weak. No one was surprised when Britain, the most powerful country in Europe, won the war.

Britain gained the island of Hong Kong and forced the Chinese to open four more ports for foreign trade. Trade between Europe and China was no longer in favor of the Chinese. When trading had first begun, the Chinese people were not interested in European made goods. However, Europe had begun using machines to weave cloth and make clothes. This made their products cheaper than Chinese handmade goods. The Chinese people bought the cheaper products. Chinese home industry was quickly destroyed, more opium was imported, and Chinese money became worth less and less.

China had many natural problems also. Years without rain were followed by sudden floods. In both cases, crops were ruined and the peasants did not have enough food to eat. A chant at that time describes the dreadful conditions: "Beans, sold by the string like pearls, rather than by the catty (1 1/3 pounds); weeds from the ponds were good food; many reduced to eating human flesh, dogs eating dogs, rats so hungry they gnawed away at nails."

Instead of helping the peasants, the Chinese government continued to force them to pay higher and higher taxes. This resulted in many rebellions in different parts of China.

The Chinese government was also having problems with Britain. It still wanted to stop the opium trade while Britain was pressing for more trading privileges. These disagreements started a Second Opium War from 1856 to 1860.

China lost again. This time England won a tiny part of China across from Hong Kong island called the Kowloon peninsula. Foreigners were also given permission to recruit Chinese laborers to go overseas to work.

As the years went by, the Chinese government became weaker, and foreign power became stronger. Life became more and more difficult for the Chinese people. After paying taxes or rent for their farms, the peasants had very little, if anything, left for themselves to eat. Some left the villages to look for jobs in the cities, but there was no work available. Finally, in order to keep their families alive, Chinese men had to go overseas to work. They left in great numbers.

2.3 Some families were so poor that they sold their girl children into slavery. This woman, Lalu Nathoy, was sold as a little girl and taken to America. She was forced to work in a saloon in Idaho for many years before she was finally freed.

Chinese Go Overseas

Chinese law did not allow Chinese citizens to go overseas to settle, but there was no law preventing them from going overseas to find work. In fact, when China lost the Second Opium War, it gave foreign powers the right to recruit laborers to work overseas.

Britain was especially interested in recruiting Chinese laborers. In 1833, Great Britain freed black slaves so the plantation owners in the British Empire wanted cheap labor. They decided to replace the freed slaves with Chinese laborers. These laborers had to sign contracts agreeing to work a certain number of years.

The first Chinese Contract Laborers (called coolies) left China in 1845. Almost all of them came from the area around the seaport of Kwangchow. In the next ten years, large numbers of these Chinese coolies went to Peru, Cuba, Hawaii, Trinidad, British Guiana, Jamaica, British Borneo and other countries.

Unfortunately, this coolie trade was almost the same as the slave trade. It quickly earned the name "pig business." Recruiters used trickery and force to make men sign the contracts. Sometimes they even kidnapped the workers they needed. They were then locked into "pig pens" and smuggled out on the first ship available.

Conditions on the ships were dreadful. As many as five hundred men were crowded into one hull so they barely had room to lie down. Due to overcrowding, lack of food, unsanitary conditions and harsh treatment, riots and murders sometimes occured and over one fourth of the laborers died on board. Many of those who lived through the voyage died soon after from the poor working conditions on the plantations and in the mines.

3.1 Chinese laborers went to work in different parts of the world.

3.2 Laborers leaving Canton.

3.3 Contract laborers arriving in Hawaii.

3.4 Those who were lucky
enough to make a lot
of money in America
often had homes built
in their home villages
in China.   This house
in Kwangtung Province
was built by a Chinese
storekeeper in Hawaii.

The Chinese government became alarmed over the coolie trade and the poor treatment of Chinese in Peru and Cuba. It sent out special investigators to inspect the actual conditions of the Chinese coolies.

Yung Wing, the investigator assigned to Peru in 1873, documented his report with dozens of photographs showing Chinese coolies whose backs were "lacerated and torn, scarred and disfigured by the lash." After his report, no more coolies were permitted to leave for Peru and Cuba.

The United States was also involved in the coolie trade. Conditions on board American ships were so terrible that the Viceroy of the Kwangtung and Kwangsi Provinces protested repeatedly to the American Envoy in China, John E. Ward, between 1860 and 1861. Mr. Ward denied everything. He claimed that although the ships were American, the recruiters were foreign nationals and he could not control their actions.

3.5 Immigrants on board an American ship, the Alaska.

However, the people of California thought the coolie trade was too much like slavery. When Californian businessmen wanted to bring in coolie labor, the citizens protested against contract labor. The businessmen still wanted cheap labor so they established the Credit Ticket System.

Under the Credit Ticket System, the employer paid the worker's passage to California. The worker then had to pay the employer back from the money he earned. The employer also took back the cost of food from the earnings, leaving the laborer with very little. Actually, this system was not much better than contract labor.

Some Chinese peasants were more fortunate. While they had to leave their homeland in order to support their families, they were able to pay their own passages in steerage by mortgaging their farm lands or borrowing money from friends and relatives. Even so, they suffered unbearably on the voyage.

The August 28, 1888 issue of the SAN FRANCISCO EXAMINER described the conditions on board the ships. "The space assigned to each Chinaman is about as much as is usually occupied by one of the flat boxes in a milliner's store. It would be a strange sight to one not accustomed to it to see a framework of shelves, not eighteen inches apart, filled with Chinese. If a few barrels of oil were poured into the steerage hold, its occupants would enjoy the distinction so often objected to, of being literally 'packed like sardines.'"

Nevertheless, the Chinese came.

3.6 Chinese immigrants arriving in San Francisco, 1878.

3.7 Chinese immigrants going through customs in San Francisco, 1875.

Gold Fields

In 1848, gold was discovered near Coloma, California. James Marshall was building a saw mill for John Sutter when he noticed bits of gold metal in the mill pond. The news of this discovery spread all over the world.

First, Americans from the East coast poured into California. Then the Hawaiians arrived, followed by South Americans. In 1849, Europeans heard the news and joined the rush to California.

The American miners did not want to share the gold with foreigners. As early as 1850, they asked the California State Legislature to pass a Foreign Miners' Tax.

This bill forced all foreign miners to pay a very high price for a mining license. After a short fight, foreign miners from Europe, Mexico and South America gave up and left the mining fields.

By 1852, the exciting news about the "Mountains of Gold" reached China and 20,000 Chinese arrived in San Francisco to prospect for gold.

The American miners who had not wanted to share the gold with the European and Mexican miners were upset at the flood of Chinese newcomers. They were glad of the services that the Chinese provided such as boarding houses, general stores, restaurants and laundries. But they did not want to share the gold fields.

The Miners' Tax had worked in getting rid of foreign miners (mostly Mexicans) in 1850 so the American miners asked the California legislature to renew the tax to exclude the Chinese from the gold fields. The legislators ignored the miners' requests.

The miners took matters into their own hands. They expelled

4.1 San Francisco before the gold rush, 1846.

4.2 San Francisco two years after gold was discovered, 1850.

4.3 Mining gold, 1850.

4.4 A Chinese mining camp.

the Chinese from the mining camps, sometimes beating and even shooting the Chinese they found.

This frightened the legislature into quickly renewing the Foreign Miners' Tax. The tax remained law until 1870. During this time, the state collected over five million dollars.

The tax, however, did not stop the violence against the Chinese miners. Fake tax collectors searched out Chinese miners to steal their gold. The real tax collectors were as bad as the fake ones, killing those who refused to pay.

One tax collector wrote in his diary, "I was sorry to stab the poor creature; but the law makes it necessary to collect the tax; and that's where I get my profit."

Chinese were not protected against this violence. The August 8, 1853 issue of the ALTA CALIFORNIA reported, "An American yesterday attacked a Chinaman, beating him shamefully. The Chinamen in the neighborhood were afraid to interfere and the Americans, of whom there was a large crowd, stood by and saw the poor Chinaman abused. The assailant held the unfortunate Celestial by the queue and kicked and beat him until he was tired, and when the poor fellow got loose and was going off a policeman came up, saw by his bloody face that he had been in a fight and arrested him."

No one knows exactly how many Chinese were hurt or murdered. However, it was so bad that most of the Chinese left the gold fields, and all Chinese immigration to California slowed down.

A few Chinese miners refused to give up. They grouped together for protection and worked the poor claims the American miners didn't want. When most of the gold had been taken from the easily worked placer deposits, American prospectors abandoned them. Chinese miners bought the old claims and worked the abandoned tailings.

The ability of the Chinese to work these mines through large scale projects surprised the American miners. Teams of workers used pine trees to build wing dams of up to two hundred yards across streams. They also developed a chain pump which was turned by a man on each side working a treadmill of four spokes on the same axle. Through this kind of team work, the Chinese miners were able to make a living where individual American miners could not.

As American miners left, Chinese miners gradually moved back and by 1870, almost one third of the miners in California were Chinese.

Chinese miners did not only work in the gold mines. They were also an important part of the quicksilver and borax mining industries in California which produced millions of dollars. However, the working conditions were terrible and ruined the health of many miners.

When the California gold fields were worked out, Chinese miners followed new gold strikes as far north as Alaska. Again, they were often expelled, hurt, and killed by the other miners. Oregon, Idaho, and Montana passed laws like the California Foreign Miners' Tax against the Chinese miners.

Nevertheless, the Chinese continued to work the poor and abandoned claims until the early 1900's when the claims were exhausted.

4.5 A quicksilver miner
with his queue wrapped
around his head.

4.6 China imported a large amount of quicksilver from the New Almaden Mine. In the early 1850's, the Emperor of China sent this pagoda (along with a crew to erect it) as a token of his appreciation.

4.7 A large scale Chinese mining project.

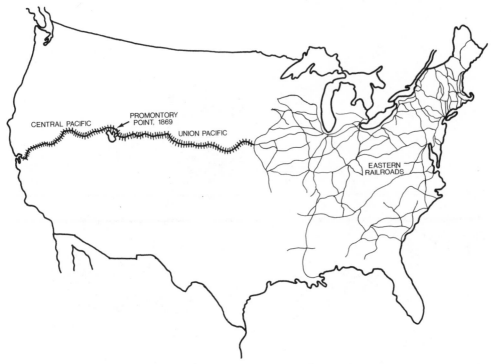

5.1 When the railroad was completed, it linked the East Coast with the West.

5.2 Chinese railroad workers, Sierra Point, Ca. 1867.

Railroads

California became a state two years after gold was discovered. There was plenty of work to be done in building the new state.

One big project was to build a railroad that would join the East Coast with the West. The plan was for the Union Pacific to lay track from the East while the Central Pacific Railroad (headed by the "Big Four" Crocker, Stanford, Hopkins and Huntington) started from the West. The government promised the railroad companies anywhere from $16,000 to $48,000 plus a grant of land for every mile of road that was constructed. This was the beginning of a great railroad race for power and profit.

At first, Charles Crocker had no problem in hiring workmen because shiploads of Irishmen were arriving in San Francisco. However, railroad work was very dangerous and exhausting. The foremen complained that the workers were often drunk and rowdy and constantly demanding higher wages. After each pay day, several hundred workers would disappear.

As a result, it took the Central Pacific two years to lay only fifty miles of track. Charles Crocker was worried. His railroad company needed to work faster but he couldn't get the laborers he needed. In 1865, Crocker's foreman, John H. Strobridge, could only get 800 laborers. He needed 5,000. Crocker told Strobridge to hire Chinese.

The Chinese already had excellent work records with another railroad company, the California Central which had hired them to replace the white workers who left for the gold mines in the 1850's. However, Strobridge refused to hire Chinese. He said, "I will not boss Chinese. I will not be responsible for work done by Chinese laborers. I don't think they could build a railroad." Governor Leland Stanford, one of the "Big Four," was also against hiring Chinese laborers. In fact, he wanted Chinese excluded from California.

Finally, Crocker was so desperate that he forced Strobridge to hire fifty Chinese as an experiment. They worked so well that 3,000 more were hired. Governor Stanford changed his attitude about the Chinese. In a report to President Andrew Johnson on October 10, 1865, he wrote, "Without them (the Chinese) it would be impossible to complete the Western portion of this great national enterprise within the time required by the Acts of Congress."

At first, most Chinese workers were recruited from the mining districts. Then contractors were sent to China to bring back more laborers. Soon, four out of five workers on the railroad were Chinese and construction moved ahead quickly.

When the railroad reached the High Sierras, the workers had many difficulties to overcome. The hardest part was to carve away big chunks of the mountains with explosives so track could be laid. But there was no place for even a foothold in the steep cliffs.

Chinese workers were lowered in baskets. They drilled holes for the explosives, lit the fuses and then swung out as far as they could to avoid the blast. Other workers quickly pulled up the ropes, but sometimes the baskets were not hauled up quickly enough, and the men were killed by the explosions. Sometimes the ropes broke, and the workers fell to their deaths.

Another problem was the snow. Entire work camps were buried to the rooftops in snow. The men burrowed through tunnels like moles. They breathed through air shafts and never saw daylight until spring. Occasionally, avalanches swept whole camps down the mountains. The bodies, still clutching their shovels, were not found until the following spring when the snows melted.

After the snows of the High Sierras came the scorching heat

32

5.3 During the winter months, Chinese continued working by tunneling through the snow.

5.4 Chinese were lowered in baskets to drill holes for explosives.

5.5 A railroad camp.

5.6 Chinese section hands working on the Northern Pacific Railroad.

of the Nevada desert. Some of the Chinese tried to leave for other work. They were beaten, whipped and forced to stay.

Others complained about unfair working conditions. The Chinese were paid $26 a month without board while the white laborers received $35 a month plus board. The white workers also worked fewer hours and they were never used for the dangerous jobs.

Finally, 2,000 Chinese workers went on strike in 1867. They demanded the same work day and wages as white workers and the right to look for other work. Charles Crocker broke the strike by forcing the Chinese to go without food and water supplies until they went back to work.

The railroad between the West and East Coasts was finished in 1869. There were huge celebrations from coast to coast. The Chinese, however, were excluded from participating and they were not even mentioned during the ceremonies.

Nevertheless, the Chinese continued to build rail links throughout California, the Southwest and the Northwest.

5.7 A placque commemorating the accomplishments of the Chinese on the Southern Pacific Railroad. The Chinese reads: A railroad in California/Linking the South and the North/(Lingers) the spirit of the Chinese/Who gave their flesh and blood.

Agriculture

Many of the Chinese immigrants had been farmers in China, so when they arrived in America it was natural for them to look for work in agriculture. Between 1860 and 1890, Chinese could be found working in every part of California's farming industry.

They labored in the vineyards in the Napa Valley of California, taking care of the grapes and digging huge storage tunnels for the wineries. Some worked as dairy and sheepmen; others became vegetable growers, migrant harvest laborers, or wood cutters. They helped start fruit growing in California; and they were also employed in the canneries where they processed the fruit and made the cans. Later, they became important as flower growers.

6.1 Drying the grape harvest.

6.2 Flower seller.

6.3 Wood cutter carrying his load of wood to sell.

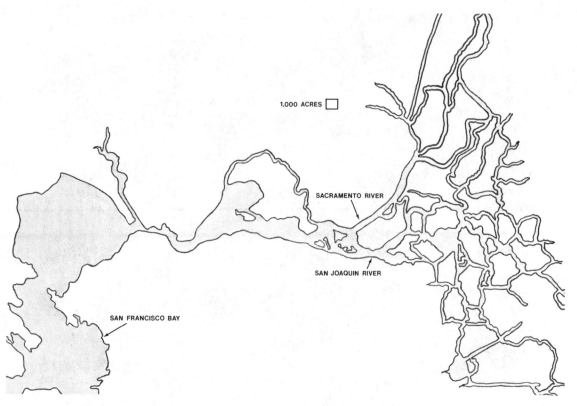

6.4 Sacramento Delta waterways and reclaimed farmland.

6.5 Chinese laborers reclaiming swamp land.

One of the first tasks the Chinese accomplished was reclaiming California's swampland. The delta region which is formed by the San Joaquin and Sacramento Rivers had very rich soil, but it was covered with water and tule marshes. The water had to be drained. Chinese laborers built endless miles of levees, ditches, dikes and canals to drain the water. By the 1870's, they had changed thousands of acres of useless swampland worth $1 to $3 per acre into valuable farm land worth $20 to $30 per acre.

After the land was reclaimed, these Chinese laborers joined the other Chinese farm workers. By 1890, the Chinese were 75% of the total agricultural labor force in California.

Most Chinese worked as field hands. They were employed as fruit pickers harvesting apples, peaches, cherries, pears, and strawberries. The PACIFIC RURAL EXPRESS, on September 16, 1893, wrote, "It is difficult to see how our annual fruit crop could be harvested and prepared for market without the Chinaman." Nevertheless, they were often poorly paid for their talent and hard work.

They did not accept the low wages without protest. There were several strikes for higher wages in the 1870's and 1880's but these were unsuccessful.

Some Chinese who were tired of the low wages became small farmers. Most rented land or worked as sharecroppers. Share-croppers paid for the use of the land by giving half the earnings from their vegetable and grain crop and three fifths of their fruit to the land owner.

Some Chinese experimented with new methods of farming. It was Chinese farmers who first tried hatching eggs by using artificial heat. And the RED BLUFF BEACON in 1870 said that the Tehama County peanuts which were grown by the Chinese were "the sweetest we ever tasted."

A few Chinese achieved fame for their new developments. Guey Jones developed a superior variety of rice which led to a prized industry in Glenn County, California. The Bing cherry is named after the Chinese farm foreman who developed it. However, the most outstanding Chinese agriculturalist worked in the Florida orchards.

Lue Gim Gong got his start while working as a strike breaker in a shoe factory in Massachusetts. On Sundays, he attended a volunteer school started by the citizens of North Adams to teach the Chinese factory workers English.

Lue was a particularly bright student. He came to the attention of Frances Burlingame who invited him to live and work in her family home. She paid for him to take courses in the regular town school and encouraged him to experiment with the fruit trees in the family orchards.

Later, when his health did not allow him to remain in Massachusetts, she bought him an orchard in DeLand, Florida. There, he developed many new and different kinds of fruit. He created currants as large as cherries, peaches that ripened in time for Thanksgiving, apples that were sweeter than the ones other groves produced and raspberries that were a strange salmon pink color.

People called him the plant wizard, and in 1911 he was awarded the Wilder Silver Medal by the American Pomological Society for his new orange. This orange could hang on a tree for more than one year and did not spoil even when it took months to get to the market.

While most Chinese farm workers did not achieve fame, the people of California depended on their labor. When the Chinese vegetable peddlers near Los Angeles went on strike in 1878, the people of Los Angeles went completely without vegetables for several weeks. And in 1884, when the first cannery was built in Sutter County, the managers did not want to hire Chinese. However, they found that they could not find anyone else who knew how to make the cans they needed, so they were forced to hire Chinese after all.

6.6 Farm workers.

6.7 Vegetable peddlers sold their produce from house to house.

6.8 Lunas, or supervisors, on a sugar plantation in Hawaii.

6.9 Chinese laborers in the cane fields in Louisiana.

In the late 1890's, Japanese began to replace Chinese in farm work. This was the time of the anti-Chinese movement and feelings against the Chinese grew so strong that it was dangerous for them to remain in the countryside where they could not protect themselves.

Many of the large ranchers and farmers watched their farms, factories and vineyards go up in flames, forcing them to get rid of their Chinese workers. Leland Stanford had the largest vineyard in the world at that time. He employed over 300 Chinese workers. Mrs. Stanford said the white workers "threatened to burn everything in sight. They commenced, and all the vineyard tools, ploughs, and so forth were destroyed. Also, three thousand tons of hay and the same amount of alfalfa." As a result, the contract with the Chinese workers was broken, and they were replaced with white men.

Some Chinese left to work in other states. Others banded together and continued going up and down the state as migrant workers. Kam Wai, a former migrant worker, said that in the 1920's, "Chinese were just like Latins are now. You could see them all over the valleys, moving by the season. For a buck and a half you could ride these little limousines that went out from Chinatown to the farm. In the beginning of the summer, you picked cherries, after that pears, after that you planted tomatoes." Others traveled by box cars from one destination to another.

After World War Two, life became easier for the Chinese in America. They left migrant farm work and were replaced by Mexican and Filipino laborers who continue to work in the fields today.

Fishing

Some of the Chinese who immigrated to California had been fishermen in China. When they were driven from the gold fields in the early 1850's, they could not find work in the towns and cities so they turned to work they knew. They grouped together and started small fishing villages. They were the first commercial fishermen in California.

Later, they were joined by other Chinese, ex-railroadmen and laborers who were driven out of the factories during the anti-Chinese movement. Chinese fishing villages dotted the coast from Baja California to San Francisco.

The Chinese caught many kinds of fish and shrimp which they salted and dried. The dried fish and shrimp were then packed into barrels, boxes or sacks and either sold locally or shipped to China, Japan and the Hawaiian Islands.

7.1 Shrimp Fishermen.

7.2 A Chinese fishing camp, Monterey, Ca., 1875.

7.3 Fishermen drying squid.

7.4 Children selling abalone shells, Monterey, Ca.

7.5 A fishing junk in San Francisco Bay.

FISHING

While fishing, the Chinese discovered abalone. At that time,
Americans did not eat abalone but the Chinese did. They caught
the abalone, salted the meat and sent it to China. When Americans
saw the pretty abalone shells, they wanted to make them into
jewelry and ornaments. Soon abalone shells became so popular
that there was a demand for them to be exported.

During the late 1850's, European immigrants started moving
into California from the East Coast in larger numbers. Among
them were Greek, Italian and Dalmatian fishermen. They resented
the Chinese in the fishing industry so they asked the California
legislature for a tax like the Miners' Tax to force the Chinese out.
The first tax law against Chinese fishermen was passed in 1860.

This law was the first of a series that made it difficult for
the Chinese to remain in the fishing industry. A law passed in the
1870's limited the size of nets the Chinese could use. Then in 1882,
a law was passed against the Chinese fishing boats called junks.
They were declared foreign vessels and banned from American
waters.

However, there were two areas in which Chinese were permitted to work undisturbed, the shark industry and the salmon canneries.

The Chinese caught sharks for the fins and a lubricating oil
from the liver. Americans had no use for either of these products
so the Chinese shark fishermen were left alone.

The Chinese worked in the salmon canneries. The hours were
long, and the work was seasonal, so white workers did not want the
jobs. Chinese continued to work in the salmon canneries until the
early 1900's when they were replaced by Japanese and Filipinos.

The rest of the fishing industry was taken over by Italian
fishermen who dominate it to this day. In fact, the only Chinese
fishing village which remains today is China Camp, a shrimp
camp in Marin County.

China Camp was started later than many of the Chinese
fishing villages. In 1882, hundreds of Chinese who could not find

work in San Francisco moved across the bay to the small cove on the San Pablo peninsula. They picked this site because of the shrimp bed located there.

They caught the shrimp in trap nets. When the shrimp was brought ashore, it was boiled for ten to fifteen minutes. Then it was spread out to dry in the sun for four to five days. Next, the shrimp meat was loosened from the shell. This was done by workers who wore special wooden shoes. After they walked on the shrimp to crush them, the shrimp was shaken in baskets to separate the shell from the meat. Sometimes, the shrimp meat was separated from the hulls by using shrimp mills patterned after the ones the fishermen had used in China. The shells were then used as fertilizer and the meat was exported.

The fishing village flourished until 1910 when the State of California introduced sea bass into San Pablo Bay as a game fish. These fish were for weekend fishermen who caught them as a hobby. The law therefore stated that these fish could only be caught on a hook and line. The Chinese trap nets caught the sea bass along with the shrimp so they were forced to stop using the nets. The fishermen left China Camp to look for other work.

Quan Hock Quock refused to leave. Instead, he invented the drag net which trapped the shrimp but released the bass. He formed his own shrimp company which soon became the major supplier of shrimp in the San Francisco Bay Area. When Quan Hock died, he left the business to his two sons, Henry and George.

After World War Two, pollution in the bay started killing the shrimp. The business shrank until all that remains is a cafe run by Quan Hock Quock's grandson, Frank. Frank serves shrimp cocktails in the cafe, rents a few row boats, and sells shrimp to fishermen for bait.

The fishing pier and a few of the stilt houses in which the Chinese lived are still there, and the camp has been made a part of the California State Park System.

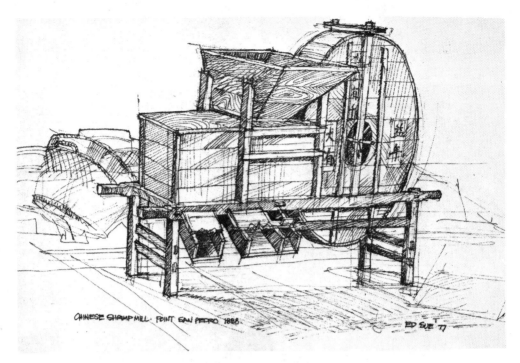

7.6 A shrimp mill modeled after those in China, Point San Pedro, Ca., 1888.

7.7 China Camp today.

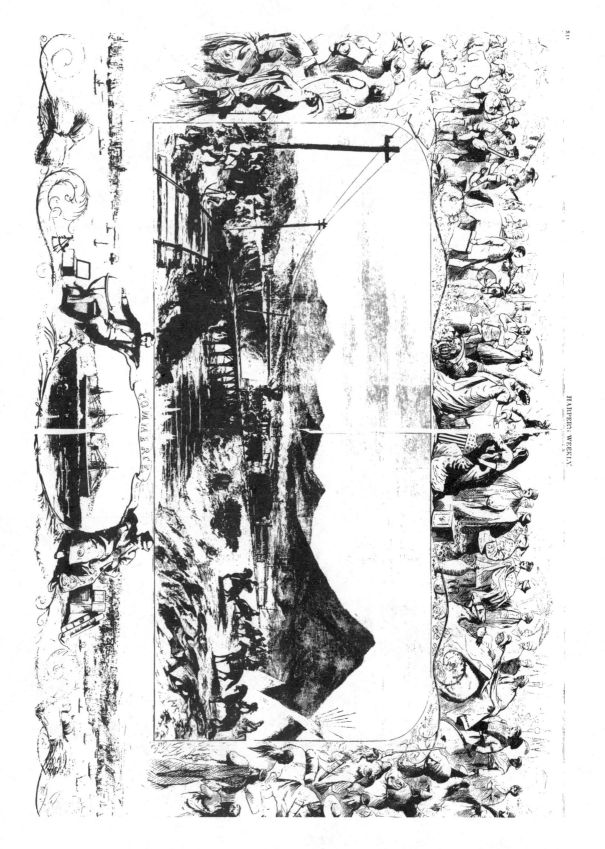

8.1 The completed Pacific Railroad was intended to link Europe with Asia across the American continent.

Maritime Industry

The Chinese seamen from the Kwangtung and Fukien provinces were well known for their skill and courage. They had navigated the oceans in their own junks for many centuries. Later, they were employed as sailors by the British East India Company. However, in the 1860's, steam power was introduced to the China seas and rivers. As a result, thousands of Chinese seamen became unemployed. Some left for the "Golden Mountains." Others went to look for work in British controlled Hong Kong. There, they soon became an important part of the China Trade.

At the same time, the American shipping industry was changing. The completion of the railroad in 1869 linked the East and the West Coasts. American businessmen hoped this would mean a faster and more profitable trade between China and America. The two most important American shipping companies in the China Trade were The Occidental and Oriental Steamship Company and The Pacific Mail Steamship Company. They shared docks and facilities in San Francisco and made at least twenty four round trip voyages to China each year.

The officers on board these ships were always white Americans but most of the crew members were Chinese. The Chinese seamen served as boatswains, firemen, coal passers, stewards, cooks, waiters, cabin boys, store keepers, bakers and pantrymen. These crewmen were hired in Hong Kong for round trips to San Francisco. When the ships returned to Hong Kong, they were discharged and new crews were hired.

Chinese crewmen were also used on American ships and steamers traveling up and down the West Coast and through the Panama Canal. In fact, between 1876 and 1906, Chinese made up more than half the crews on board American ships.

The Seamen's Union was angry about the large number of Chinese crewmen because they believed the Chinese were lowering the wages and working conditions for American sailors. Actually, the companies had two pay scales. Seamen hired in Hong Kong were paid $7 to $15 per month while those hired in American ports were paid $25 to $55.

Nevertheless, the Seamen's Union joined the Representative Assembly of Trades and Labor Unions on the Pacific Coast in 1882. The purpose of this assembly was to remove Chinese workers from all American industries, including shipping. The assembly urged Congress to pass the Chinese Exclusion Act which would make it illegal for American steamship companies to hire nonresidents in American ports. After the Exclusion Act was passed, however, the West Coast steamship companies continued to hire Chinese crewmen. The Seamen's Union protested. The shipping companies pointed out that their crews

8.2 Chinese seamen unloading lumber from the American ship, the Guy C. Goss.

were hired in Hong Kong for round trips, so the Exclusion Act did not apply to them.

Before the Exclusion Act, Chinese seamen, like those from other countries, could petition to become American citizens. After the act passed, this was no longer possible. In order to enter America, some Chinese seamen jumped ship.

The regulations restricting Chinese crewmen therefore became increasingly rigid. In 1884, Chinese seamen were forced to carry a white tag for identification if they wished to leave their ship. Later, the steamship companies were required to post bonds when Chinese seamen went ashore. By the 1890's, there were so many restrictions that the companies finally had to provide living accomodations on the docks for their Chinese crewmen.

The Seamen's Union continued to pressure for more legislation against Chinese crewmen. Finally, in 1915, the Federal Seamen's Act improved the working conditions on board ships in order to attract more American seamen. At the same time, the act reduced the number of Chinese, Japanese and Filipino seamen until they almost disappeared from American ships.

Early California Industries

California's opportunity to develop industries came during the Civil War (1861-1865) when factories on the East Coast could not keep up with the demands for products.

The factories had to manufacture weapons, ammunition, and other war related items as well as the usual necessities for the civilian population, such as clothing and household goods, but they were short of labor because most able bodied men were in the army.

Some of the early industries in California were woolen mills, cigar factories and factories that made slippers. One of the main sources of workers for these factories was the Chinese immigrant.

Just as the industries in California were beginning to grow, the Civil War ended. Thousands of soldiers were released from the army. Also, the factories that were manufacturing war goods closed. This meant that there were a large number of unemployed men looking for work, forcing wages to become lower. By 1867, all of America was affected by a terrible, post-war economic slump.

The manufacturers on both the East and the West Coasts used cheap immigrant labor to keep costs low and profits high. After the Civil War, manufacturers on the East Coast continued to employ European immigrants, but the American unions on the West Coast forced manufacturers to lay off the Chinese immigrants and hire American workers.

The boot and shoe industry was just starting in California. The firm Buckingham & Hecht refused to pay American workers the wages they demanded so the workers went on strike. The firm hired Chinese to break the strike. The Chinese learned the work quickly, and other boot and shoe factories started hiring them.

9.1 A Chinese cigar factory on Merchant Street, San Francisco.

9.2 A Chinese boot factory.

THE HISTORY OF AN INTERLOPER.

Ah Sin's Curiosity.

Far away from his country and kin
From Canton came the guileless Ah Sin.
   As he watched men make shoes,
   He exclaimed "What's the use.
They won't hire me," but still he stepped in.

Crispin Instructs Him.

But the foreman just wanted a hand,
Few white men were then in the land;
   And the placid Ah Sin
   Went to work with a grin,
And a smile that was childlike and bland.

His "Bludda" is Introduced.

Soon another Chinee comes along—
The humble and patient Ah Hong—
   With the awl and the last,
   He learns just as fast,
And his labor he gives for a song.

A White Minority.

And so they came in by the score,
While the white men went out at the door,
   While the Melicans napped,
   Their cheap pupils were apt;
And the foreman is left now—no more.

The Last of the Crispins.

For a while the white workman held on
To the bench, where he first had taught John,
   Till at last he is 'fired'
   By Ah Sin—whom he hired—
And the last of the Crispins is gone.

Master of the Situation.

Ah Sin has grown wealthy and great,
And he shipps boots all over the State,
   From the white man he learned,
   A pile he has earned.
And his teachers must now emigrate.

As the economic situation improved, the other industries began to rehire Chinese in large numbers. Soon, Chinese made up three fourths of the total work force in mills in San Francisco, Stockton, Sacramento, and Marysville, and more than half the cigars and footwear manufactured in California were made by Chinese.

Californian manufacturers prevented strikes and controlled wages in different ways. For example, white female workers were paid as little as the Chinese, so mill owners cleverly mixed the female workers in with the Chinese who could not speak English. Since neither group could communicate with the other, this prevented both the Chinese and the women from getting together to organize any effective strikes.

American boys were paid even less than the Chinese, so when the Chinese workers in the footwear industry went on strike, the employers broke the strike by advertising for American boys to take their places.

Then a second recession struck in 1875. Factories closed and workers filled the bread lines. Manufacturers and union bosses quickly blamed the Chinese for the economic slump, and a large number of Chinese workers were laid off once again.

Some Chinese began their own footwear and cigar factories. In order to survive, they posed as American and Spanish firms by using false names such as F.C. Peters and Co., and Cabanes & Co. They also hired American salesmen, but the workers inside the factories were all Chinese.

In the footwear industry, the Chinese factories made inexpensive shoes, while the American ones made the more expensive shoes and boots, so there was little competition between the two.

The cigar industry, however, was the scene of a bitter struggle between the Chinese and American factories. The cigars made in the Chinese factories were the same quality as those made by Americans but they sold at a lower price. The American unions were furious and called for a boycott of Chinese made cigars, but the smoking public could not tell the difference between American made and Chinese made cigars. Then Samuel Gompers, an union leader, had the idea of placing bands, like rings, around American made cigars. Americans stopped buying Chinese made cigars, and the Chinese owned cigar factories went out of business.

The recession of 1875 was so serious that Californian industry never recovered from it. Eastern manufacturers had the advantages of a steady supply of cheap labor from Europe and large amounts of capital and fuel. The intercontinental railroad made it easy for them to send their products to the West Coast where they were able to undersell California made goods. As a result, the woolen, cigar and boot industries in California gradually disappeared.

CELESTIAL CUBANS.

To make seed Havanas
By covert addition
Of dry cabbage leaves
Is the Coolie's ambition.

And these are the weeds
That our exquisites smoke.
"White Labor Cigars"—
'Tis a very good joke.

9.4 & 9.5

Continuing Industries

There were three industries that survived the economic recession of 1875. These were industries that fulfilled basic needs: the sewing industry, restaurants, and laundries.

Many Chinese worked in the garment industry. A San Francisco newspaper in 1873 reported: "Next, if not superior in importance to the Chinese cigar factories, are the Chinese clothing factories of which there are altogether 28, including 3 shirt factories... These factories employ from 50 to 100 men each and their employees number in aggregate about 2,000."

The garment trade was divided into three main areas: male clothing and tailoring; shirts, ladies' garments and undergarments; and overalls. The workers for each area came from a specific part of China and formed their own labor guild. These guilds regulated the hours and the conditions of work. They made sure that all the Chinese workers in the garment industry were paid the same amount for the same work.

At the beginning of this century, Chinese women who arrived in California started working in the sewing trades. However, the garment guilds did not allow women to join their organizations. As more and more women entered the industry, and men began to retire or find work elsewhere, the guilds lost their power, and by 1930 only one guild remained.

Since that time, there have been several attempts to unionize the workers effectively. In 1938, two hundred workers in the largest garment factory in San Francisco's Chinatown protested against the practice of using part-time shifts and demanded a nine-hour, full-time work day. When the owner refused, the workers voted in favor of union representation and went on strike for fourteen weeks.

These workers formed the first Chinese chapter of the International Ladies Garment Workers Union. A contract was finally signed giving the workers their demands, but this turned out to be a hollow victory. The factory was owned by the National Dollar Store chain which decided to move the operations to Los Angeles, so the workers ended up jobless.

Another attempt to better working conditions by striking was made in 1968. Twelve workers of a Chinatown factory that contracted work from Margaret Rubel Co. had been working fifty to sixty hours a week, but their employer forced them to show only forty hours on their time cards. They demanded an union shop. The workers were fired. Nevertheless, with the support of the International Ladies Garment Workers Union, they were able to picket the factory for four weeks. At that time, the owner closed the factory rather than give in to the workers' demands. This forced the women to find jobs elsewhere. Though the women later won a court settlement from Margaret Rubel Co. for back wages, this kind of an experience has discouraged further attempts to unionize the workers.

Today, most of the workers in the small Chinatown garment factories are older immigrant women who cannot speak English and therefore cannot get jobs outside of Chinatown. The factory owners are usually Chinese who speak enough English to contract for work from larger American factories. The contractors who charge the least get the most work, so they compete with each other by giving low bids. This stiff competition and the lack of a worker organization has resulted in the Chinese women working twelve to fourteen hour days doing piecework for about fifty cents an hour.

However, many of the women need the flexibility that doing piecework allows. They are permitted to work irregular hours and leave when necessary to take care of their children. Besides, even those who are dissatisfied need the money too desperately to go without work very long.

10.1 Two women picket against unfair working conditions.

10.2 A Chinese restaurant in San Francisco.

10.3 A Chinese restaurant on Dupont Street, San Francisco.

The early Chinese immigrants had a similar problem. They soon discovered that, in order to get work, they would have to agree to be paid less than American workers for the same job, or to take jobs white men were not interested in. Many longed to have their own businesses where they could have some control over their own lives even though being self-employed often meant working even longer hours for less money.

During the gold rush in California, the Chinese found that the two greatest needs were for good food and clean clothes. The Chinese therefore chose to start businesses in these two areas. The need was there; they required very little capital to start; and they would not be in direct competition with American business-men.

The Chinese opened restaurants in the cities, mining camps, and later in the railroad camps. At first, the restaurants served only Chinese food. Then they began adapting some Chinese dishes to American tastes, thus developing Americanized Chinese food such as chop suey and fortune cookies. They also began serving American dishes. The restaurants became extremely popular and their popularity has continued to this day.

Laundry up to this time had been washed by Mexican and Native American women or sent to Hawaii or Canton to be done. This latter method took two months, and it was so expensive that it was almost cheaper to buy a new shirt than to have it washed.

The Chinese laundry industry started in 1851 and grew quickly. In 1876, San Francisco contained some 300 laundries, and almost every town in California had at least one.

The owners formed a guild to govern the industry and protect its members from competition among themselves and from unfair laws. During the 1870's and 1880's, when many Americans wanted the Chinese to go back to China, San Francisco refused to give Chinese licenses to operate laundries and passed laws that condemned the Chinese wash houses. The guild fought these laws in the courts and won.

In 1933, over 3,200 Chinese laundry workers and the owners of small laundries in New York city organized the Chinese Hand Laundry Alliance. This group also fought successfully against discriminatory legislation.

NOTICE TO OUR PATRONS

San Francisco, June 1, 1917

DURING the past six months the cost of all materials used in the Laundrying of clothes—such as soap, starch and soda—has increased to such an extent that it is impossible for us to continue doing Laundry work for our patrons at our former rates.

The cost of these materials is constantly advancing. Owing to this fact, in order to exist and continue in business, it is absolutely necessary that we advance our prices and charge more for Laundry work than heretofore, much as we regret having so to do.

We trust that our patrons will realize the necessity that compels us to take this step, and will continue to favor us with their patronage in the future as in the past, and assure them that when conditions again become normal, we will be pleased to reduce our prices and charge accordingly.

Very respectfully,
THE CHINESE LAUNDRIES.

10.4 All the Chinese laundries in San Francisco raised their prices at the same time because of the Laundry Guild.

10.5 Inside a Chinese laundry.

In addition to the restaurants and laundries, some early Chinese immigrants recognized a need for stores to sell provisions to the men in the gold mining camps. They started small general stores which were very successful. When the railroad started, other Chinese opened stores in the railroad camps and nearby towns. These stores served both Chinese and American workers.

Today, Chinatowns are crowded with small groceries, antique, jewelry, and import shops for both residents and tourists.

10.6 A Chinese store, 1904.

10.7 The window of a Chinese barbershop.

10.8 (Below) Chinese men had to visit the barbershop once a week to have the fronts of their heads shaved.

10.9 A cobbler.

10.10 A pipe bowl mender.

10.11 An herbalist.

10.12 A grocery store.

10.13 Restaurant workers trying to unionize the Mandarin
Restaurant in San Francisco.

However, the wages of workers in Chinese restaurants, laundries, and shops are generally very low while the hours are long (9 to 10 hours a day). There are two reasons for this.

The owners know that their shops are popular largely because of the low prices. In order to keep the prices down, they have to pay the workers poorly and be content with a small profit. Many of the laundries, restaurants and shops survive because they are family owned, and members of the family work for no pay.

In the case of the larger restaurants and shops, these are usually owned by Chinese-Americans or by foreign investors. Like the sewing factories, these owners often take advantage of the large number of Chinese immigrants who cannot speak English and therefore cannot find jobs outside of the Chinatowns. They pay the workers as little as $350 a month for fifty hour work weeks. If the workers question their employers about working conditions, they take the risk of losing their jobs.

In 1972, twenty busboys, waiters and waitresses were fired from their jobs at Asia Garden, a large restaurant in San Francisco, for this very reason. The workers picketed the restaurant and filed a lawsuit against the employer for unfair labor practices. After a month, the employers were finally pressured into rehiring fifteen of the workers.

However, owners know that most of the immigrants cannot go that long without pay. Because of this, most strikes and demands for higher wages and better working conditions in the Chinatown businesses have failed. Thus the cycle of hard work and low wages for new immigrants in these industries is still continuing.

Anti-Chinese Movement

San Francisco welcomed the first Chinese immigrants. These immigrants came as merchants of independent means, or they worked as laborers, cooks, domestic servants and tailors. As they were few in number and almost none of them went into the gold mining districts, Californians did not feel threatened by the Chinese.

In fact, Chinese were allowed to live and start businesses anywhere. They were also included in all important state celebrations such as Admissions Day, Washington's Birthday, and Independence Day. The Chinese were part of the parades, and when the politicians made speeches, they praised the Chinese as clean, industrious, and desirable workers.

The reaction of American businessmen was so enthusiastic that, in 1852, California's Governor John McDougal recommended a system of land grants to persuade more Chinese to immigrate and settle in California.

That was the same year that 20,000 Chinese arrived in San Francisco to join the gold rush. Thus, at the same time that Governor McDougal was suggesting bringing in more Chinese, the gold miners were trying to exclude the Chinese from mining in California and yelling "California for Americans." Because of the miners' actions, Chinese immigration dropped within three years to only 3,329 in 1855.

However, when California needed laborers to build the railroad and to reclaim swampland recruiters were sent to China to persuade laborers to come to California. This encouraged Chinese immigration, and during the 1860's, 12,000 Chinese arrived in

California every year, working wherever there was a need for their labor.

Americans expected the Chinese to go back to China after the railroad was completed and the swampland reclaimed. Instead, these Chinese remained and more Chinese arrived in the 1870's.

Conditions in China had steadily worsened. Government officials, landlords, and bandits all preyed on the peasants. Sometimes, parents would even have to sell one of their children into slavery in order for the rest of the family to live.

Most of the young men in the Pearl River Delta of Kwangtung tried to leave their villages for America. Often, as many as 30% of the men in one village would be working overseas in order to support their families in the village.

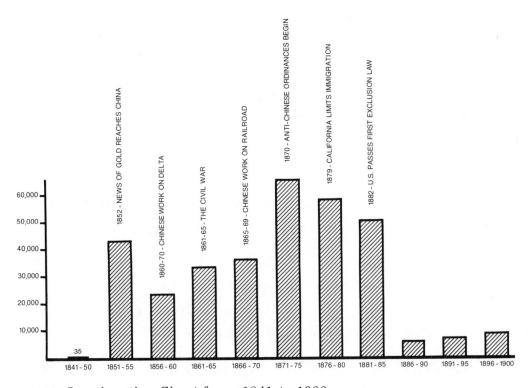

11.1 Immigration Chart from 1841 to 1900.

The Chinese were able to work for less than the American laborer because their families were in China, and the money they sent home was worth a lot more in China than in America. The management of the factories took advantage of this and paid the Chinese men the same as they paid American women and children. This was much less than the American male workers who wanted wages that would allow their families in America to live well. As long as there was plenty of work for everybody, the employers hired American men and paid them more than the Chinese. But changes were occuring which altered the economic picture.

Industry was beginning to change from small sweatshops that used a lot of labor to modern factories that needed fewer workers.

At the same time, the Californian manufacturers were competing with the Eastern manufacturers who had plenty of cheap labor from Europe. Employers started hiring more Chinese laborers who would work for less than the American workingman.

The situation became critical when America went into a depression that reached from coast to coast. The California Comstock Lode, which had for many years seemed an endless source of silver and gold, was drying up. This caused the stock market in San Francisco to plunge.

Then the Bank of California went broke in 1875. This set off a financial panic that shook California's economy from top to bottom.

Job competition became fierce and many employers took advantage of the situation and lowered wages. Workingmen ended up either unemployed or working for less than they could live on.

The American workers became desperate. They formed labor parties such as the Workingmen's Party of the United States and the Workingmen's Party of California which was led by Denis Kearney, a very persuasive speaker.

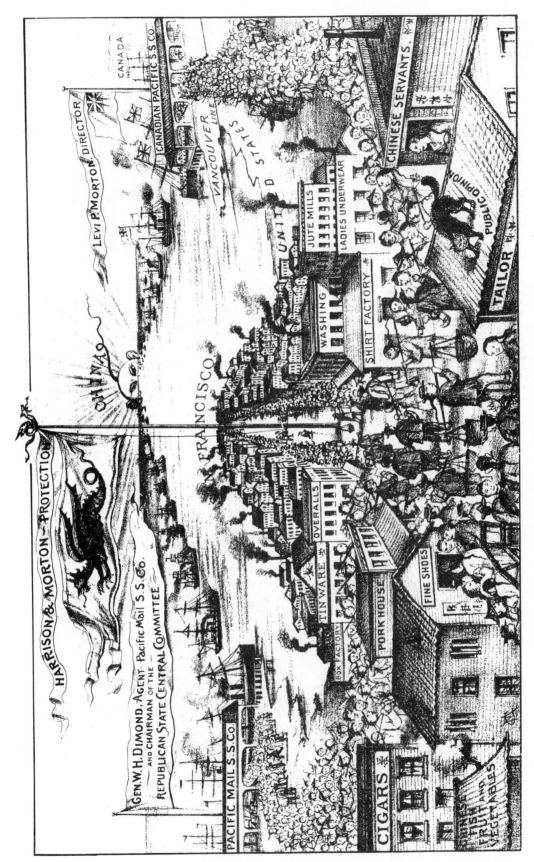

11.2 Newspapers and magazines accused the Chinese of monopolizing all the businesses.

11.3 The Workingmen's Party slogan was "The Chinese Must Go."

11.4 A pro Workingmen's Party cartoon.

These political parties were formed to fight for better working conditions and more jobs for American workers. Though American women and children were working for as little (and sometimes less) than the Chinese workers, the political parties only blamed the Chinese for holding down the wages and living standards of American working men. They told the workers that the only way to improve their lives was to stop the Chinese from working in California.

The workers' parties warned the big companies not to bring any more Chinese to California, and they asked the government to pass laws against the Chinese. They wanted the Chinese to be forced out of the United States. Their slogans were "Chinese must go!" "Yellow Peril," and "Chinese Menace."

The newspapers fanned the anger of the workingmen. In 1873, the SAN FRANCISCO CHRONICLE wrote, "Who have built a filthy nest of iniquity and rottenness in our midst? The Chinese. Who filled our workshops to the exclusion of white labor? The Chinese. Who drives away white labor by their stealthy but successful competition? The Chinese."

11.5 Editors fanned the workingmen's anger.

"OUT OF THE FRYING PAN INTO THE FIRE".

11.6 Almost every issue of the WASP carried an anti-Chinese cartoon.

The politicians wanted the workingmen's votes. They were glad to use the Chinese who could not vote as their scapegoat. They blamed the Chinese for California's economic problems. They started passing laws against the Chinese.

Since most of the Chinese in California lived in San Francisco, many of the early anti-Chinese laws were passed as local city ordinances. Some of these were:

THE SIDEWALK ORDINANCE (1870) which prohibited people who used poles to carry merchandise from walking on the sidewalk.

This ordinance was directed specifically against the Chinese since all non-Chinese used wagons or carts to carry heavy loads.

THE CUBIC AIR ORDINANCE (1871) required each adult to have at least 500 cubic feet of living space.

Since Chinatown consisted of only seven square blocks, there was severe overcrowding. Sometimes as many as ten or twelve people were jammed into single rooms so hundreds of Chinese were jailed for breaking this ordinance. Finally, the jails became so crowded that the Chinese accused the government of breaking the same ordinance and it was repealed.

THE QUEUE ORDINANCE (1873) forced all prisoners in city jails to have their hair cut so it was not more than one inch long.

Under Manchu law, Chinese men were required to comb their hair into single long braids called queues, so it was very humiliating for Chinese to have their queues cut off.

THE LAUNDRY ORDINANCE (1873, 1876) ruled that anyone who carried laundry without using wagons drawn by horses would have to pay a high license fee.

The legislators hoped to drive the Chinese out of the laundry business with these laws but they failed.

The Chinese fought these laws in the courts, and all of the anti-Chinese laws ended up being declared unconstitutional. Judge

Steven J. Field warned the city against passing "hostile and spite-ful" legislation, but more and more anti-Chinese ordinances were passed, and the laws remained legal for longer periods of time.

However, the Chinese had more than unfair laws to deal with. The American workingmen were not satisfied with angry speeches and anti-Chinese laws. They did not realize that when Chinese workers were driven out of the factories, the factories were often forced to close, putting even more American workers on the bread-line. All they knew was that their families were going hungry because they didn't have jobs. This drove them to violence.

Gangs of roughnecks began attacking any Chinese they saw on the streets. It became popular to catch Chinese and chop off their queues. Many hoodlums wore these "pigtails" on their belts and caps.

The police usually looked the other way. But, in July of 1871, they were forced to act when thousands of unemployed workers rioted in San Francisco's Chinatown. They robbed and killed many Chinese and burned their homes and businesses. It took three days before the police managed to stop the riot.

11.7 The San Francisco Police Department Raiding Squad, 1890's.

Charges were pressed against only a few of the hoodlums. Even these culprits were set free. Chinese were not allowed to testify against white men in court, so there were no witnesses to convict the rioters.

The anti-Chinese movement spread state-wide in 1879 when California drew up its Second Constitution. Laws were included to limit Chinese immigration to California. The Constitution also made it unlawful for corporations to hire Chinese, and Chinese were not allowed to work in the government. The Governor even declared March 4, 1880 as a legal holiday for anti-Chinese demonstrations.

Labor leaders called on men to "take up arms and enforce the law of the state." Mrs. Ann Smith, chairperson of the Workingmen's Committee, said, "They call us a mob. It was a mob that fought the Battle of Lexington, and a mob threw the tea overboard in Boston Harbor, but they backed their principles... and you should do the same. I want to see every Chinaman - white or yellow - thrown out of this state."

The violence spread all through the Western States. When a white man was killed in a police raid in Los Angeles' Chinatown, a huge mob destroyed Chinese houses and businesses. They killed at least 22 Chinese including women and children. They also hung 50 persons from the lamp posts by their queues.

In 1886, one of the largest anti-Chinese riots took place in Seattle, Washington. An anti-Chinese committee for Washington State demanded that all Chinese in the area leave by a certain day. The Grand Jury indicted the members of the committee but they were acquitted.

These members of the committee, aided by the acting Chief of Police and nearly the entire police force, led a group of men with wagons into Seattle's Chinatown. They forced the Chinese to pack their belongings and drove them to the docks to be loaded on a steamship bound for San Francisco.

Some white citizens tried to help the Chinese. They organized a "Home Guard" and fought to prevent the mob's actions. President Cleveland was forced to call in the National Guard and several rioters were killed. It was months before security was fully restored.

11.8 The anti-Chinese riot in Seattle, Washington.
1. Driving the Chinese onto the steamer.
2. Marching under guard to the courthouse.

Other riots occured in Nevada, Colorado, and Montana. In 1885, 28 Chinese were murdered and many others seriously wounded in a massacre in Rock Springs, Wyoming, a coal mining center.

In the same year, 32 Chinese miners were murdered in their sleep in Douglas Bar, Oregon. The Chinese government demanded an investigation, and three men were arrested and charged with murder, but they were later acquitted.

11.9 The massacre of Chinese at Rock Springs, Wyoming.

Chinese were evicted from Tacoma, Truckee, Antioch, Eureka, Juneau and many other cities. It became almost impossible for them to find work on the West Coast. Finally, 200 Chinese who were desperate for work agreed to be sent to the East Coast as strike breakers.

Other Chinese tried to escape the violence in the West. They did not go back to China because that meant almost certain starvation for their families and themselves. Instead, they scattered all across America, and by 1890 Chinese could be found in every state in the union.

The American workers in the Midwest and on the East Coast became afraid for their jobs. They began to support the working-men's parties in the West and the anti-Chinese movement became a national issue.

11.10 The Chinese being expelled from Eureka.

Exclusion Laws

During the 1860's, when California needed Chinese labor, the United States wanted to maintain good relations with China. American diplomats negotiated the BURLINGAME TREATY with China in 1868.

This treaty agreed to Chinese immigration to America and American immigration to China. It gave the same privileges and freedoms for immigrants to either country.

In the 1870's, America no longer needed or wanted Chinese labor, but there was a large number of Chinese immigrants arriving in San Francisco every year. The American workingmen's parties pressured the United States Congress to stop Chinese immigration.

12.1 Chinese immigrants arriving in the 1870's were often stoned.

Congress passed a FIFTEEN PASSENGER BILL which prevented any ship from carrying more than fifteen Chinese immigrants. President Hayes refused to sign the bill because it went against the Burlingame Treaty which promised Chinese that they could come to America freely.

The American workers then demanded the repeal of the Burlingame Treaty. The anti-Chinese movement became so strong that the Burlingame Treaty was changed in 1880 to allow the United States government to limit Chinese immigration. This was the first time in the history of the United States that one group of people was picked out for limited immigration.

The American workers continued to pressure Congress to pass more laws against Chinese immigration. The EXCLUSION LAW of 1882 permitted teachers, students, merchants, and tourists to enter the United States, but it stopped the immigration of laborers for ten years. It also stated that no Chinese could become a naturalized American citizen.

12.2　After the Exclusion Law passed, Chinese merchants like
　　　these were still permitted to enter America.

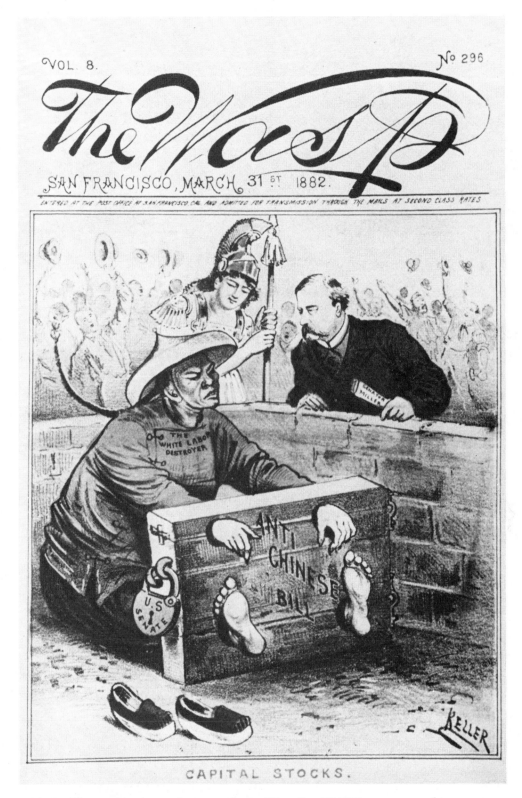

12.3 Newspapers and magazines like the WASP pressured
Congress to pass anti-Chinese legislation.

WHEREAS:- Lun Sing, a Chinese Merchant of Tonopah, Nye County Nevada. Is about to depart for China, intending to return, now therefore for the better identification of the said Lun Sing and to further facilitate his landing upon his said return, we the undersigned, citizens and residents of Tonopah, precinct Nevada, being duly sworn, each for himself depose and say, they are personally acquainted with the aforesaid Lun Sing, that he is not a laborer, but a Merchant in good standing and of the firm of Wah On High & Co., of Tonopah, Nevada, said firm consisting of How On Tong and Lun Sing, and they further depose and say that have known the said Lun Sing, as a Merchant of Tonopah, for the ten months last past.

County of Nye,   )
State of Nevada.   ) S.S

On this   day of   personally appeared before me a

          in and for the said County of Nye, L. G. Cushman, C. M. Smith and G. A. Kerrick, each for himself deposes and says that the statements above are true and correct.

                              Subscribed and sworn to before me
                              this   day of   1902.

                              Notary Public, in and for the
                              County of Nye, State of Nevada.

12.4 Chinese leaving America for visits back to China had to carry re-entry papers like these.

86

Chinese immigration dropped drastically after the Exclusion Law was passed. More than 40,000 Chinese had immigrated to America in 1881. Only ten entered in 1887.

Congress also passed the SCOTT ACT (1888) which stopped any Chinese worker who had left America from returning to the country. At that time, about 20,000 Chinese had gone home to China for visits. They were not allowed to return even though they had re-entry papers.

In the same year, the King and Legislature of the Hawaiian Kingdom passed an ACT TO REGULATE CHINESE IMMIGRATION. Chinese were no longer permitted to land in Hawaii unless they possessed a permit granted, signed, and sealed by the Minister of Foreign Affairs. Again, these permits were only given to non-laborers. This law was modified in 1895 to permit employers to import Chinese laborers, provided they would also bring in one European or American laborer for every ten Chinese permitted to enter. However, the United States Government made no such modifications. In fact, the laws became stricter.

The 1882 Exclusion Law was so effective in stopping Chinese immigration that the American workers pressured Congress to renew it. Congress extended the law for ten more years with the GEARY ACT (1892).

This act also required Chinese to apply for a certificate of eligibility in order to remain in the United States. If approved, they were issued a "photo passport" which they had to carry at all times.

This act resulted in daily harrassment for the Chinese who could be stopped at any time and forced to produce their certificate. If they did not have it, they would be detained until someone could be found to bring the certificate or vouch for them.

A San Francisco newspaper, the CHUNG SAI YAT PO, complained that teachers, merchants, their wives and children, and students of high official families were often detained and humiliated. A methodist minister, Ng Poon Chew, was arrested as a laborer, tried and ordered deported, with the immigration officials insisting that a preacher was a laborer.

America reinforced the Exclusion Laws by signing a new treaty with China in 1894. This treaty prevented any Chinese laborer from coming into the United States unless his family already lived here. It also required all Chinese in America to register.

Chinese immigration almost stopped entirely when laws passed in 1902 and 1904 extended the Exclusion Laws for an indefinite period of time. However, conditions in China had not improved, and many Chinese were still anxious to come to America if at all possible. Finally, the Chinese found a loophole through which they could enter America.

A big earthquake in San Francisco in 1906 destroyed almost all the official birth records. Many Chinese took this opportunity to claim United States citizenship by saying that they were born in San Francisco, but the earthquake had destroyed their records. Other Chinese then claimed to be the family of these "American born citizens" and were therefore able to enter America. These immigrants were called "paper fathers and sons."

The IMMIGRATION ACT of 1924 stopped all Chinese women who were not the wives of merchants, teachers, students, and tourists from entering the United States. Since Chinese could neither bring their wives from China, nor marry American women, few Chinese babies were born in America. As a result, the Chinese population which had started to drop with the first Exclusion Laws, decreased even further.

The Chinese continued to fight those unfair laws in court. Although they won many cases and some of the laws were repealed, they still lost most of their rights, and the Exclusion Laws remained legal and were strictly enforced.

12.5 San Francisco City Hall after the earthquake of 1906.

12.6 Some Chinese tried to enter the United States through Canada.

13.1 The shed on the Pacific Mail Steamship wharf.

13.2 Angel Island Immigration Station.

Angel Island

The Exclusion Laws permitted certain Chinese to immigrate to the United States. However, the process which they had to go through in order to enter America was an ordeal designed to discourage them from coming.

During the 1800's, all persons entering the United States (immigrants and citizens) had to have their papers checked. They also had to be examined by doctors to make sure that they were not ill or carrying any contagious diseases. This process usually took a few hours except for the Chinese immigrants.

After the Exclusion Laws passed, Chinese arrivals were forced to wait for days, weeks, and sometimes even months before they were questioned by immigration inspectors. In the meantime, they were detained in an overcrowded wooden shed at the Pacific Mail Steamship Company Wharf on the San Francisco waterfront.

The Chinese community leaders protested this poor treatment of immigrants, but neither the Chinese nor the American government did anything to change the situation.

The Commissioner General of Immigration visited the shed in 1902. The terrible conditions shocked him. He immediately asked for money to build a better detention center. He suggested building the new Immigration Station on Angel Island, a small island in the middle of San Francisco Bay.

The Chinese in America protested. Keeping immigrants on Angel Island meant a great deal of inconvenience. Witnesses would have to take a whole day off in order to give a few minutes of testimony. Also, the forty-five minute boat ride was dangerous in foggy and stormy weather.

The authorities ignored the protests. The detention center was built on Angel Island. It was completed by 1909 at a cost of $200,000.

After the completion of the Immigration Station, all arrivals to San Francisco were immediately transferred from the passenger liners onto a small steamer which took them to Angel Island. Again, immigrants of all nationalities except for the Chinese, were released from the island after a few hours.

Chinese immigrants usually had to stay at least three or four weeks. Many remained for months. Some were kept on the island for two and even three years while their cases were being decided in the courts.

The processing for the Chinese began with physical examinations. Chinese were forced to go through tests for hookworm and liver flukes. No other immigrant group was tested for these parasites.

Even worse than the tests, the immigrants had to take off all their clothes and stand naked in front of each other while waiting for the doctor to examine them. This was extremely embarrassing and humiliating for the women who were used to Chinese doctors who never asked their patients to undress.

After the physical exam, they were marched to the barracks. There were two barracks, one for the men and one for the women. Each barrack was just a large, bare room with long rows of bunks in two, sometimes three tiers.

The bathrooms had no privacy. The toilets were all in one row with no dividers. Some women protected each other's privacy by covering their faces with paper bags before going up the stairs to the bathroom.

Each barrack also had a tiny, closet-size, windowless room used for solitary confinement. If an inmate became upset to the point of hysteria, refused to obey orders, or was found breaking a rule, he or she would be locked in this room.

13.3 The dining hall, Angel Island.

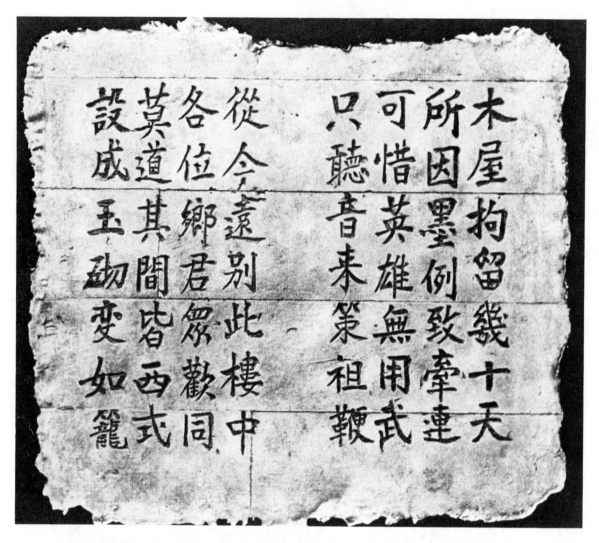

設成玉砌變如籠　莫道其間皆西式　各位鄉君眾歡同　從今遠別此樓中　只聽音來鞭祖鞭　可惜英雄無用策　所因墨例致牽連　木屋拘留幾十天

13.4 Two poems written on the walls of the barracks on Angel Island.

From this moment on, we say goodbye to this house,
My fellow countrymen here are rejoicing like me.
Say not that everything is western styled.
Even if it were built with jade, it has turned into a cage.

Several scores of days detained in this wood house
All because of some inked rules which involved me.
Pity it is that a hero has no way of exercising his power.
He can only wait for the word to whip his horse
  on a homeward journey.

Translated by Hsu Kai-yu
Three Generations of Chinese - East/West
Oakland Museum, 1973.

Meals were served in the dining hall. The men and women had separate meal times so they could not meet and talk. Even husbands and wives were not allowed to see or talk to each other.

Once inside the barracks, there was nothing to do except wait until the interrogation officer was ready to question the immigrant. Some men passed the time by gambling. Some women knitted or sewed. Others read the few Chinese newspapers and books that were available.

Though the immigrants could see San Francisco through the barred windows, they were not allowed to see or talk to relatives and friends who lived there. In fact, they were treated just like prisoners.

Some immigrants became so unhappy that they killed themselves. Many expressed their misery by carving poems on the wooden walls of the barracks with forks and spoons smuggled out of the dining hall.

The walls of the barracks are still covered with poems like this one.

> Why do I have to sit in jail?
> It is only because my country is weak and my family is poor.
> My parents wait at the door in vain for news;
> My wife and child wrap themselves in their quilt,
>   sighing with loneliness.
> Even should I be allowed to enter this country,
> When can I make enough to return to China with wealth?

The Chinese knew the kinds of questions that they would be asked. These questions were different from those asked immigrants from other countries. They were about small details regarding their homes and villages in China. They were therefore extremely difficult to answer.

For example, they were asked, "How many steps are there up to your house in China?" "What is your bedroom floor in China made out of?"

The immigrant was asked the question first. Then a witness from San Francisco was asked the same questions. If the answers were different, the immigrant was either deported back to China or the case might be appealed to Washington, or go to court to be decided.

The interrogations often lasted more than one day. Some went on for three days. The immigrants were so nervous that they sometimes completely forgot what they had memorized and gave the wrong answers. The interrogations were held through interpreters because the immigration officials could not speak Chinese, and the immigrants could not speak English.

It was so difficult to pass the interrogations that there were many cases where relatives and friends of the immigrants bribed the interrogators and interpreters to make sure the immigrant could enter the United States. There were several scandals as a result of these bribes. The biggest scandal was in 1917 when 25 immigration officers were dismissed, transferred or forced to resign.

The Commissioner General visited Angel Island in 1922. He said the buildings on Angel Island were filthy firetraps unfit for human beings. His comments were ignored and the immigration station continued to be used until 1940 when the administration building burned down.

After the Immigration Station was abandoned, the buildings were left to fall apart in the damp, foggy weather. A few burned. The only building that remains is the one that housed the barracks for the men and women.

In August 1974, pressure from Asian Americans persuaded the California State Assembly to call for the establishment of a China Cove Historical Citizens' Committee. This committee made recommendations to the State Director of Parks and Recreation for preserving the last remaining building.

13.5 The Immigration Center of Angel Island.

13.6 & 13.7 The barracks
on Angel Island today.

FOR JUSTICE—
For Chinese,
American Friendship

WRITE, WIRE
Your CONGRESSMAN Today
Asking Him To Support The

REPEAL of the CHINESE
EXCLUSION ACT!
Congress Convenes September 13th

SUPPORT . . .

Resolutions supporting the repeal of the act were recently passed by the following organizations:

American Legion, California Dept.

Veterans of Foreign Wars, California Dept.

California Council, CIO

Oregon Council, CIO

San Francisco Chamber of Commerce

Houston Chamber of Commerce

Portland Chamber of Commerce

Seattle Chamber of Commerce

Houston Foreign Trade Association

Citizens For Victory Committee

Y. W. C. A. Business Girls Conference (California)

Chinese Christian Youth Conference (Tahoe Conference)

The City of San Francisco

Legislation to Repeal Chinese Exclusion

There are several bills before Congress which aim to repeal the Chinese Exclusion Laws, place Chinese immigration on a quota basis, and permit the Chinese to become naturalized citizens.

Proponents of these measures are urging the passage of this legislation for three reasons:

1. As a measure of war expediency, to strengthen Chinese morale.

2. As an act of overdue justice to a friendly people against whom humiliating discriminations have been made.

3. As a means of cementing the good will of a great nation with whom post war trade will be highly profitable.

Only those things which are just and right will, in the long run, prove expedient.

Following is a list of members of the Immigration Committee of the House of Representatives. Write to Chairman Samuel Dickstein and members of the Committee as possible. In addition to your local Congressmen. Letters should be addressed to Immigration and Naturalization Committee, House Office Building, Washington, D. C.

Samuel Dickstein, N. Y., Chairman; John Lesinski, Mich.; Lex Green, Fla.; Dan R. McGehee, Miss.; A. Leonard Allen, La.; John L. McMillan, S. C.; Robert Ramspeck, Ga.; Ed Gossett, Tex.; Thomas J. Scanlon, Pa.; O. C. Fisher, Tex.; Noah M. Mason, Ill.; Edward H. Rees, Kans.; Carl T. Curtis, Nebr.; Hubert S. Ellis, W. Va.; Bernard W. Kearney, N. Y.; William P. Elmer, Mo.; John B. Bennett, Mich.; Lowell Stockman, Oreg.; Edward O. McCowen, Ohio; and J. R. Farrington, Hawaii.

You Can Help Right Now! What To Do

If you believe in supporting the democratic principles on which this country was founded, and righting the unjust laws which discriminate against the Chinese, you can help right now. Will you help? This is what you can do.

1. Let your Congressman know that you are in favor of this legislation. Write him a letter, or send him a telegram.

2. Write letters to the newspapers expressing your views, and urging the repeal of Chinese exclusion.

3. Inform people around you of the issue.

WHOM TO WRITE:

Listed below are the names of the senators and representatives of the states and cities most populated by Chinese. Petitions to be sent or wired should be addressed to the Senators or Representatives at the Senate or House of Representatives respectively in Washington, D. C. It is your duty to voice your opinion on this most vital legislation to your Congressman TODAY.

SENATORS

Arizona: Carl Hayden, D.; Ernest W. McFarland, D. California: Hiram W. Johnson, R.; Sheridan Downey, D. Illinois: Scott W. Lucas, D.; C. Wayland Brooks, R. Massachusetts: David I. Walsh, D.; Henry Cabot Lodge Jr., R. Michigan: Arthur H. Vandenberg, R.; Homer Ferguson, R. New Jersey: Albert W. Hawkes, R.; W. Warren Barbour, R. New York: Robert F. Wagner, D.; James M. Mead, D. Oregon: Charles L. McNary, R.; Rufus C. Holman, R. Texas: Tom Connally, D.; W. Lee O'Daniel, D. Washington: Homer T. Bone, D.; Mon C. Wallgren, D.

REPRESENTATIVES

Arizona: John R. Murdock, D.; Richard F. Harless, D. California: (San Francisco) Thomas Rolph, R.; Richard J. Welch, R.; (Oakland) Albert E. Carter, R.; John H. Tolan, D.; (Santa Rosa) Clarence F. Lea, D.; (Nevada City) Harry L. Englebright, R.; (Stockton) J. Leroy Johnson, R.; (San Jose) Bautista) John Z. Anderson, R.; (Fresno) B. W. Gearhart, R.; (Tulare) A. J. Elliott, D.; (Santa Barbara) George E. Outland, D.; (San Dimas) Jerry Voorhis, D.; (Los Angeles) Norris Poulson, R.; Thomas F. Ford, D.; Will Rogers Jr., D.; Cecil R. King, D.; (Hollywood) John M. Costello, D.; (Long Beach) Ward Johnson, R.; (Montebello) Chet Holifield, D.; (Pasadena) Carl Hinshaw, R.

(... remaining states ...) Illinois; Massachusetts; Michigan; New Jersey; New York; Oregon; Texas: (Dallas) Hatton W. Summers, D.; (Houston) Albert Thomas, D.; (San Antonio) Paul Kilday, D. Washington: (Seattle) Warren G. Magnuson, D.

D stand for Democrat, R for Republican.

SUGGESTED FORM LETTER

Dear Sir:

For freedom and equality China fights in this World War II against our common enemy Japan. She needs freedom and equality from members of the United Nations too!

As representative of our State, your support of the bills pending in Congress before the Immigration Committee, having for its purpose the repeal of the Chinese Exclusion Act, will be deeply appreciated.

Very truly yours,

This Ad Sponsored by
Friends of China
and Advocates
of Justice

14.1   After America and China became allies the Chinese Press urged its readers to write to Congress for the repeal of the Exclusion Laws.

New Immigration Laws

After the Japanese bombed Pearl Harbor in 1941, the United States became an ally of China. This changed American foreign policy, and the Chinese Exclusion Acts were repealed in 1943.

As a result, Chinese could become naturalized American citizens. Also, 105 Chinese were allowed to immigrate to the United States each year.

During World War Two, many American servicemen in China married Chinese women. The WAR BRIDES ACT (1945) allowed these wives of American servicemen to enter the United States. About 6,000 Chinese women came through this act.

14.2 Chinatowns all across America gave generously to the War Chest.

14.3 Some Chinese-American women joined the WAAC.

14.4 Chinese American veterans formed their own chapter of the American Legion.

After World War Two, civil war broke out in China between the Nationalists and the Communists. The American government was strongly opposed to communism at home and abroad. It supported the Nationalists. The Communists won and the Nationalists were forced to escape to Taiwan.

The American government refused to recognize the Communist government in China and Congress passed new immigration laws to help the refugees.

The DISPLACED PERSONS ACT (1948) gave permanent resident status to 3,465 Chinese students, visitors, and seamen who did not want to go back to China.

The REFUGEE RELIEF ACT (1953) allowed 2,777 refugees from China to enter America. 2,000 additional visas were given to Chinese refugees.

Some Chinese who did not like the Communist government in China went to Hong Kong. Hong Kong became overcrowded. President Kennedy signed a special PRESIDENTIAL DIRECTIVE (1962) which permitted over 15,000 refugees to enter the United States immediately.

American immigration laws at that time followed a quota system which allowed a large number of Europeans to enter the United States every year. Only a small number of Asian immigrants were permitted entry. In 1965, President Johnson signed a new immigration law which abolished this system.

This new act said that starting July 1, 1968, each independent country outside of the Western Hemisphere would be allowed to have 20,000 of its citizens immigrate to the United States each year. Each person would be considered according to his country of birth, not his nationality or race.

This law has allowed thousands of Chinese to immigrate to America in the last ten years. Persons born in China enter as refugees. Those born in Hong Kong, a British Colony, are counted against Great Britain's quota of 20,000.

Under the immigration act, the Chinese born in Hong Kong cannot use more than 200 of the 20,000 visas alloted to Great Britain each year. There is therefore a long waiting list of Hong Kong born Chinese waiting for American visas. Some families have waited decades in order to come to America to join husbands and fathers who have spent all their adult years in this country.

Chinatowns

When the Chinese first came to America, they could live any-where. However, they often chose to live in the same area so they would be around people who were familiar and who spoke Chinese. Later, when the violence against the Chinese began, they moved closer together for mutual help and protection. China-towns thus formed and grew.

The circumstances surrounding Chinese immigration were different from those of other immigrant groups. These differen-ces had a profound effect on the structure of the Chinatowns.

The Europeans usually immigrated as a family, or the men came first and sent for their wives and children as soon as pos-sible. The Chinese men usually came alone and were seldom joined by their families.

The European countries are very small. All the immigrants from one country spoke similar dialects of the same language, ate similar kinds of food, and practiced similar customs. China is a very large country and though most of the Chinese immigrants came from Southern China, they often spoke completely different dialects, so that persons from different districts could only under-stand each other with difficulty. Moreover, they practiced distinct variations of the same customs.

The United States did not pass any laws affecting European immigrants until 1917. However, in 1882, Congress passed laws which restricted the lives of Chinese already in America.

The result was the formation of Chinatowns that were uniquely different from any of the European communities. One of the big-gest differences was the lack of women and children.

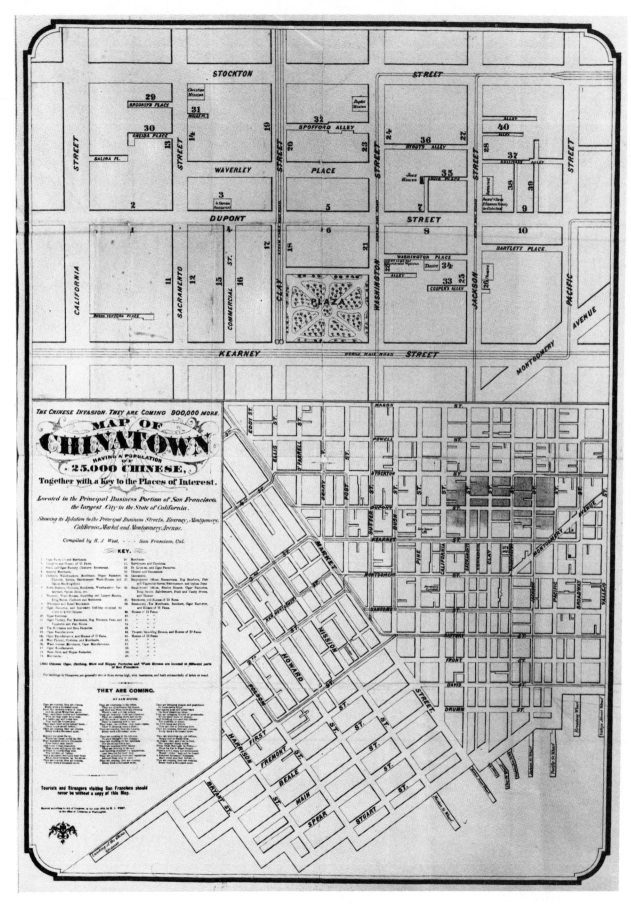

15.1 A tourist map of Chinatown in 1873.

15.2 San Francisco Chinatown a hundred years ago.

15.3 New York Chinatown today.

The Chinatowns in America between 1850 and 1940 were "bachelor societies." At first, this was because most of the Chinese who came to America in the 1850's and 1860's did not intend to make their homes here. Many came with contracts for a specific period of time. Others thought that they would get rich quickly in the "Mountains of Gold" and then go home to China to retire.

The laborers soon discovered that it would take many years to make the money they needed to go home and live a life of comfort. They also realized that while the money they earned went a long way in China, it was not enough to bring their families to join them.

15.4 Most of the laborers were illiterate so they paid letter writers to write letters home.

Even the merchants who had the money were reluctant to bring their families because of the violence of life in the West. Besides, Confucian beliefs encouraged the women to stay home in order to take care of their parents-in-law and perform ancestral worship.

Then, the Exclusion Laws stopped the wives of laborers from joining their husbands in America. The laws also discouraged the wives of merchants from coming.

As one Chinese merchant put it, "When my little boy came to this country, he was kept in the immigration office for over two months. Poor little fellow - he was so homesick. That is the reason why my wife hates to come over here. It would break her heart to have to stay so long in the immigration office."

In any case, the Immigration Act of 1924 stopped most Chinese wives from joining their husbands. As a result, the marriages and family life for the average Chinese in America were very much like that of Wing Yee's grandparents.

Wing Yee's grandfather came to America, worked hard, saved his money and returned to China to get married. The Exclusion Laws prevented him from bringing his wife back to America with him.

An uncle brought their son, Wing Yee's father, to America. When he grew up, there was no way for him to marry in America. There was only one Chinese woman for every nineteen men, and the laws forbade his marrying a non-Chinese. So he returned to China to marry even though he knew the Exclusion Laws would prevent him from returning with his wife.

Their son, Wing Yee, came to America when he was twelve. In 1935, he returned to China to marry. Since the Exclusion Laws were still in effect, he could not bring his wife back with him. Finally, the new immigration laws allowed his wife and daughter to join him in 1948. His daughter, who wasn't even born when he left China in 1936, was twelve years old!

Obviously, it was almost impossible for the Chinese in America to have any kind of family life. Most of the men endured lonely existences, with only the hope of the future to sustain them.

The men earned very little money, and almost everything they earned was either sent home to their families, or saved so that they could return to China for a visit. Usually, it took ten or more years to save enough for a visit home. After the Scott Act which forbade Chinese laborers who left America from returning, even these visits were stopped.

Some tried to escape their loneliness by taking drugs. Others tried to get rich faster by gambling. Sometimes they lost everything they had struggled for. Even those who saved every penny of their earnings often could not save enough for retirement. They died in America, and only their bones made the journey home to China for burial.

15. 5 Cleaning the bones of the dead.

15.6 One of many Chinese night schools in San Francisco, Ca.

15.7 An early Chinese public school.

Since the Chinese could not establish families and thereby set down roots in America, there was no need for them to learn more than a minimum amount of English. They could not socialize with non-Chinese so there was no reason to learn Western customs.

They therefore kept their own language, customs and traditions. These were passed on to the few Chinese born in America by establishing evening Chinese schools which the children attended at night after going to segregated American schools during the day.

15.8 Traditionally, Chinese did not educate their daughters. There is only one girl in this 1890 class.

The Chinatowns became minature cities. The men built temples for worship and theatres for entertainment. They started newspapers. In fact, they tried to **re-create** in America the China they had left behind.

15.9 A Chinese actor.

15.10 The Weaverville Temple is the oldest Chinese temple in America that is still in use today.

15.11 Inside the Weaverville temple.

15.12 A Chinese New Year Parade in Boise, Idaho, 1911.

15.13 Officers of the Chinese Six Companies.

In China, whole villages were usually related to each other and had the same surname. The village elders maintained law and order.

This structure was adapted to life in America. The men with the same surnames grouped together to form "clan" associations. These separate clan associations combined together to form "district" associations.

When Chinese newcomers came to America, they looked up friends and relatives through the district associations. Those who were already here took care of the newcomers by providing them with food, housing, and information about work.

As more Chinese came to America to look for work, the associations became larger and more complicated. They became big companies which looked after the economic and social well-being of the Chinese.

The associations had specific responsibilities for their members. They acted as judges and courts when arguments occurred. They were used as banks. They helped take care of all business deals. They started and operated schools and hospitals. They took care of the funerals for members who died without friends or relatives in America.

The Chinese Consolidated Benevolent Association, better known as the Chinese Six Companies, was formed in order to bring together the biggest family associations, thereby uniting the Chinese. The Six Companies became the leader of the entire Chinese community. It represented the Chinese in fighting the discriminatory laws against the Chinese. It became the liaison between the Chinese in America and the governments of China and the United States.

Chinatowns across America have grown and changed since the arrival of wives and families in the 1940's. They are no longer bachelor societies depending on the family associations for help, strength and familial ties.

The population of the Chinatowns today are a mixture of the old time "bachelors" who have been cut off from their families in China forever because of the Communist government in China; second and sometimes third generation Chinese-Americans who are often more "American" than "Chinese;" and new immigrants who arrive each year eager for the opportunities the United States offer.

Increasingly, American born Chinese and immigrants who have become familiar with life in America leave the confines of the Chinatowns to become a part of the larger American society. The result is that the Chinatowns are, by and large, becoming places to return to for holidays and special celebrations or stopping off points for immigrants seeking to learn English and adapt to American ways.

There are many Chinese-Americans who say that while Chinatowns are glittering tourist attractions, they are also over-crowded ghettos with the same problems of other minority communities in America: unemployment and underemployment, drugs, juvenile delinquency, severe health problems, and inadequate housing and social welfare services.

15.14 Chinatown's first demonstration for better housing conditions in 1968.

15.15 A tenement kitchen.

15.16 A family of eight shares this two room apartment.

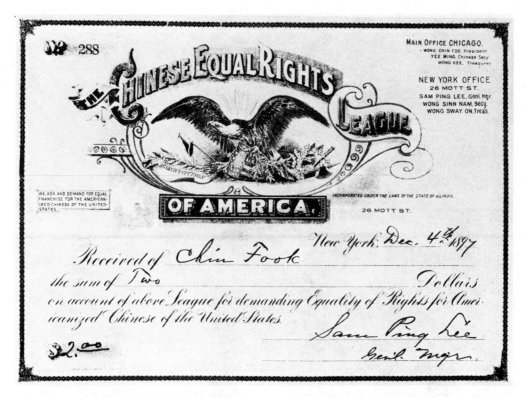

15.17 Membership receipt for the Chinese Equal Rights League.

15.18 Volunteers registering new voters in Chinatown.

The Chinese Six Companies, made up of the older, more conservative members of the communities, refuses to acknowledge the seriousness of the problems in the Chinatowns. It also does not want to give up its old, traditional ways. There are therefore some Chinese-Americans who say that the Chinese Six Companies is no longer able to meet the needs of the Chinese-American communities today.

As early as 1912, the Chinese-American Citizens Alliance was incorporated in order to oppose discrimination, gain civil rights, and better the lot of the Chinese in America. This organization has grown into fourteen chapters throughout the United States. Nevertheless, it is not a strong civil rights organization on a national scale. Nor does it speak authoritatively for all Chinese. Instead, Chinese-American communities depend on local groups to serve their needs.

One such group is the Chinese for Affirmative Action which was formed in 1969. Its purpose is to deal with some of the problems of Chinese-Americans in San Francisco's Bay Area which has the largest concentration of Chinese in the United States. This organization tries to make sure that there is equal employment for Chinese-Americans. It also defends the civil rights of Chinese-Americans and pressures for necessary social, economic, and political change.

The Chinese for Affirmative Action urges Chinese-Americans to register to vote and become a part of the political process. However, many Chinese-Americans are reluctant to become politically involved because of the fear and feelings of helplessness that were instilled in them during the period between the first Exclusion Law in 1882 and the latest immigration law in 1965.

During the period of the Exclusion Laws when the Chinese population decreased and scattered all across the United States, the Chinese realized that the only way to survive was to avoid problems by becoming as invisible as possible. This meant avoiding any social or political activity that would draw attention to them.

Then, during the 1950's, the FBI, Senator Joseph McCarthy and others in the American government raised the cry of "Yellow Peril." At that time, America was involved in the Korean War. Though the war took place in Korea, America was actually fighting Chinese Communists.

J. Edgar Hoover, the head of the FBI, charged all Chinese in America with being "susceptible to recruitment (by Chinese Communists) through ethnic ties or hostage situations because of relatives in Communist China."

These kinds of accusations were of the same nature as the ones that had led to the internment of Japanese Americans in concentration camps during World War Two. In fact, Chinese-Americans were threatened with the possibility of internment in the same camps that had held the Japanese. They were also threatened with the loss of their citizenships, deportation, and a "confession program."

The confession program was an attempt by the Justice Department to deal with the many Chinese who used false papers after the San Francisco earthquake in order to enter the United States. The program urged Chinese who had falsely claimed American citizenship to come forward and confess. They were promised "the maximum relief possible under existing laws and regulations." However, this "maximum relief" was up to the Justice Department. Not only could the "confessee" still be prosecuted, but so could relatives, friends and acquaintances. This created a web of suspicion that remains in many Chinese-Americans today.

Recent immigrants cannot vote. They also have a language barrier and their main concern is survival in a new country. Even after they become citizens, they are often afraid to "cause trouble" in case it will affect their status as citizens. They are also afraid that any problems may spoil the chances for relatives who may wish to immigrate in the future.

Nevertheless, younger members of the communities are becoming increasingly outspoken. More and more Chinese-

Americans are registering to vote and making their concerns
known by forming political groups such as the Chinese Democratic and Republican Clubs. Others are forming groups to fight
for social change. Some of these are the Chinatown Housing
Coalition, The Chinatown Committee for Better School Facilities,
etc. And the Federal Government, by creating agencies like the
Chinese Newcomers Service, is slowly beginning to respond to
the needs of Chinese-Americans and Chinese immigrants.

15.19 Chinese artifacts have been found in diggings at Langtry,
       Texas; Tuscon, Arizona; and Yreka, Donner Pass, and
       Ventura, California. Here, young Chinese-Americans
       are digging for artifacts in Hawaii.

Achievements

Most of the early Chinese immigrants were poor, uneducated coolies. All they had to offer was their strength and willingness to work. Their collective labor built the railroad which connected the West Coast with the East; reclaimed useless California swampland, turning thousands of acres into valuable farmland; started the fishing industry; and helped build up other industries.

The Chinese had a long tradition of reverence for learning. In China, a scholar was more highly respected than a rich man. The new immigrants therefore encouraged their children to make full use of the American system of free education.

At the beginning of this century, students from China sometimes came to do graduate studies at the universities in America. Some stayed and became American citizens.

As a result of hard work and study, there have been many individual Chinese-Americans who have achieved nationwide recognition and success.

Some have become outstanding educators. Gilbert Yee was born in San Francisco, but like many children from Chinatown, he did not learn to speak English until he was in public school. Now he is a fifth grade teacher in Fremont, California. He was chosen as California's top public school teacher in 1977.

Professor T. Y. Lin was born in China. He came to study engineering at the University of California at Berkeley and stayed to become a part of the faculty. He became a pioneer in pre-stressed engineering and won three national awards for his achievements.

ACHIEVEMENTS

Professor Lin started an engineering firm which is based in San Francisco but has affiliates all over the world. The firm uses concrete that is twice as strong as old fashioned concrete, and it also uses steel that is seven times stronger than ordinary steel.

Two of Professor Lin's many accomplishments are the San Francisco International Airport's elevated roadway and the Sequoias Building which fills an entire block on Geary Street in San Francisco.

There have been many famous Chinese-Americans in the field of physics. Dr. Chen Ning Yang and Dr. Tsung Dao Lee won the Nobel Prize for physics in 1957. They broke an universally accepted physical "law" - the principle of the conservation of parity. The NEW YORK TIMES compared this discovery to the "final realization that the earth was not flat."

Dr. Chien Wu, a professor of physics at Columbia University, was the experimental physicist who conducted the necessary experiments to prove Dr. Yang and Dr. Lee's theory.

Dr. Samuel C. C. Ting discovered a new sub-atomic particle and won the Nobel Prize for physics in 1976. Dr. Ting attended the University of Wisconsin. He has done research at Berkeley, Columbia, and Switzerland, and he is now a research professor at the Massachusetts Institute of Technology.

Other Chinese-Americans have made a name for themselves in law and politics. William D. Soo Hoo became the first Chinese-American mayor when he was elected mayor of Oxnard, California. Harry Low is a Superior Court Judge in San Francisco. March Fong Eu is California's Secretary of State. Perhaps the most famous of all is Hawaii's retired senator, Hiram Fong.

Hiram Fong's parents immigrated from China to Hawaii. They were illiterate so they worked on the sugar plantations. Despite many hardships, Hiram succeeded in working all the way through to graduation from Harvard Law School. He then went into private practice and became a millionaire.

16.1 March Fong Eu.

16.2 Judge Tang being sworn in.

Hiram worked hard for Hawaii to become part of the United States, and when Hawaii was admitted to the Union in 1959, he was elected as Hawaii's first member in Congress. He served four terms before retiring.

Judge Thomas Tang is another prominent Chinese-American who rose from humble beginnings. In 1910, his father immigrated to Phoenix, Arizona where he started a grocery business.

Thomas was the oldest of nine children. His college education was broken by two wars. During World War Two and the Korean War, he served in the United States Artillery Corp.

After the Korean War, Thomas began his delayed career and eventually became prosecutor of Maricopa County in Arizona, assistant Arizona State Attorney General, Maricopa County Superior Court Judge, and President of the State Bar of Arizona.

In November 1977, he was appointed to the Ninth U.S. Circuit Court of Appeals. This judgeship is second only to the United States Supreme Court and is the highest ever attained by a Chinese-American.

16.3 Hiram Fong.

Some Chinese-Americans have chosen the field of fine arts. Wah Ming Chang is a self-taught, creative, and resourceful sculptor who had several one man shows on both the East and the West Coasts before he was ten years old.

Wah Ming Chang has created puppets, movies, masks, models and monster suits and is responsible for many of the monsters on television's STAR TREK and OUTER LIMITS.

He created the special effects for THE TIME MACHINE which won an Academy Award in 1960. He also won the Golden Eagle Award from the Council on International Non-Theatrical Events for his film WANTED ALIVE which is about endangered species.

It has been difficult for Chinese-Americans to break into the movie industry, but one person who achieved incredible success in this field was James Wong Howe.

16.4   A portion of the exhibit honoring James Wong Howe. These pictures are from his early professional years, around 1920.

ACHIEVEMENTS

James was born in China and came to America as a boy in 1904. His father was a railroad store keeper. First, James tried a career as a boxer, but he was too short and soon gave that up. He then moved to Hollywood where he learned photography and became one of the top cinematographers in the world. During the last twenty years that he worked, he was the highest paid man in his profession.

James Wong Howe was nominated for an Oscar sixteen times and won it twice for THE ROSE TATTOO in 1955 and HUD in 1964. His last film was FUNNY LADY and he died in 1977, mourned by all of Hollywood.

Anna May Wong was another Chinese-American who was successful in the movie industry. She was born in Los Angeles' Chinatown in 1907. She had six brothers and sisters and her father was a laundryman so there wasn't much extra money to go around. Many of the students at Los Angeles High School earned money by working as extras in films. Anna did too. Her first role was as one of 300 extras in THE RED LANTERN (1919), but within 10 years she was playing lead roles. By 1942, when she announced her retirement to work for the USO and United China Relief, she had acted in over 100 films! She was only 54 when she died of a heart attack in 1961.

Not many Chinese-Americans have chosen careers as authors. Nevertheless, there are a few who have achieved nationwide recognition for their work.

Jade Snow Wong was born in San Francisco. Her father owned a sewing factory. She attended Mills College with the help of a scholarship. After she graduated, she surprised everybody by becoming a ceramist. No one expected someone with a college education to end up working with her hands! Her ceramic work has been displayed in museums and won many awards.

However, Jade Snow Wong is best known for her book FIFTH CHINESE DAUGHTER which tells about what it was like for her to grow up in San Francisco's Chinatown in the 1930's. Her latest book, NO CHINESE STRANGER, tells about her struggles to begin a career, her tour of the Far East as a representative of the United States, and her visit to China in search of her roots.

Two other Chinese-American authors have achieved recent success. Maxine Hong Kingston teaches at the University of Hawaii, and her book WOMAN WARRIOR won the 1976 Best Non-Fiction Book of the Year Award. Her book tells about her experiences as a Chinese-American growing up in Stockton's Chinatown.

Laurence Yep got started in writing when his high school teacher in San Francisco promised any student an A if he could get something published in a national magazine. Laurence earned the A by writing a science fiction story which was published in a magazine.

His first book SWEETWATER was also science fiction. His second book DRAGON WINGS was inspired by an article he read about a Chinese-American who created a flying machine at the beginning of this century. The book won two prizes, the Newberry Honor Book and The Promising Novel of 1975.

Though the population of Chinese-Americans is still small compared with other minorities, its percentage of achievers remains high. Other famous Chinese-Americans include: Fung Joe Guey who in 1909 flew the first aircraft on the West Coast; Sing Kee who was awarded the Distinguished Service Cross for extraordinary heroism in action in World War One; Professor Tai King Lee, master magician; Wing F. Ong, Arizona State legislator; Dong Kingman, artist; Frank Chin, playwright; Ieoh Mung Pei, the American architect chosen by Jacqueline Kennedy to design the John F. Kennedy library; Dr. Cho Mao Li, biochemist; and many, many, more.

No doubt there will be even more famous Chinese-Americans as new opportunities open up. Perhaps one of them will be Maureen "Peanut" Louie who has won the Northern California Golden Gate

16.5 In 1909 Fung Joe Guey built and flew the first aircraft on the West Coast.

16.6 Laurence Yep.

16.7 Professor Lee performing a magic trick.

ACHIEVEMENTS

Class A women's singles tennis title for four straight years and
who plans to enter the pro ranks soon; or Michael Lowe who at
23 is already a principal dancer with the Oakland Ballet Company;
or Daven Chun of Hawaii who set the World Marathon record in
1975 for the ten to eleven year olds with a time of 2:52:09; or
Kenny Fong, the eight year old chess whiz who won first place in
the U.S. Open Chess Tournament in August, 1975 in the category
of age ten and under.

When Judge Tang was being interviewed by the United States
Senate for his appointment as Judge of the Ninth U.S. Circuit Court
of Appeals, he said that anything is possible in America.

He began, "I am led to ask the question - What is a Chinaman
doing here? It has never happened before."

He went on to explain that he used the word "Chinaman" to
emphasize the change that has taken place in America since the
time when a Chinese person could not even be a witness in a court
of law. Now he was being appointed to a judgeship second only to
the Supreme Court!

"Surely," he concluded, "This is a part of the American
Dream at work."

Reading List

Chu, Daniel, and Chu, Samuel. PASSAGE TO THE GOLDEN
GATE: A HISTORY OF THE CHINESE IN AMERICA TO 1910.
New York: Doubleday, 1967.

> This history focuses mostly on the China Trade and the
> Chinese contributions to building the railroad.

Molnar, Joe. SHERMAN: A CHINESE AMERICAN CHILD
TELLS HIS STORY. New York: Watts, 1973.

> Through many photographs, and a brief text, Sherman, a
> ten year old tells what it's like to be a Chinese-American
> living in a New York suburb.

Pinkwater, Manus. WINGMAN. New York: Dodd, 1975.
Dell, 1976.

> The story of a New York boy, Donald Chen, and a
> Chinese superman, Wingman, who takes him on a ride
> to China.

Yep, Laurence. DRAGON WINGS. New York: Harper, 1975.

> A prize winning historical novel about two Chinese
> immigrants, a boy and his father, who try to fulfill their
> dream of creating a flying machine in San Francisco in
> the early 1900's.

Illustration Credits

The following photographs are courtesy of:

The Bancroft Library: 2.2, 3.5, 3.7, 4.1, 4.2, 4.3, 4.4, 5.2, 6.1, 6.2, 6.6, 6.7, 7.1, 7.2, 7.3, 7.4, 8.1, 9.1, 9.3, 9.4, 9.5, 10.2, 10.3, 10.5, 10.6, 10.10, 10.11, 10.12, 11.2, 11.4, 11.5, 11.6, 11.7, 11.8, 11.9, 12.1, 12.2, 12.5, 12.6, 15.2, 15.4, 15.5, 15.8, 15.9, 15.10, 15.11, 15.13, & the back cover.

The California Historical Society: 3.2, 5.6, 10.9, 11.3, 13.3, 14.3, 15.6, & 15.7.

Philip Choy: 13.6 & 13.7.

Ed Gray: 16.2.

The Hawaii State Archives: 3.3 & 6.8.

The Hawaii Chinese History Center: 3.4 & 15.19.

Connie Hwang: 10.13.

The Idaho Historical Society: the front cover, 2.3, & 15.12.

The New Almaden Museum: 4.5 & 4.6.

The Oakland Museum: 11.10, 12.3, 12.4, & 13.4.

The Peabody Museum: 7.5 & 8.2.

John L. Rink: 7.7.

The San Francisco History Room, San Francisco Public Library: 3.6, 6.3, 10.4, 10.7, 10.8, 14.2, 15.1, 15.15, 15.16, & 15.17.

Ed Sue: 7.6.

The United Front Press: 5.3, 5.4, 6.5, 9.2, 10.1, & 14.1.

Index

ORDER FORMS

Please send copies of "An Illustrated History of the Chinese in America" as follows:

_____ copies of the Hardback @ $11.95 each plus $1.00 shipping.

_____ copies of the Paperback @ $6.95 each plus $1.00 shipping.

California residents add 6% sales tax.

I have enclosed a check or money order for $ _____

Name: _____

Address: _____

_____ Zip: _____

DESIGN ENTERPRISES OF SAN FRANCISCO
P.O. Box 27677
San Francisco, California, 94127

- -

Please send copies of "An Illustrated History of the Chinese in America" as follows:

_____ copies of the Hardback @ $11.95 each plus $1.00 shipping.

_____ copies of the Paperback @ $6.95 each plus $1.00 shipping.

California residents add 6% sales tax.

I have enclosed a check or money order for $ _____

Name: _____

Address: _____

_____ Zip: _____

DESIGN ENTERPRISES OF SAN FRANCISCO
P.O. Box 27677
San Francisco, California, 94127